GOOD NEWS

FOR YOUR
MARRIAGE

A Gospel-Centered Guide
to a Victorious Marriage

ART THOMAS
FOREWORD BY ROBIN THOMAS

GOOD NEWS

FOR YOUR MARRIAGE

A Gospel-Centered Guide
to a Victorious Marriage

FIRST EDITION

ART THOMAS

KAINOS PUBLISHING
Romulus, Michigan

K
K A I N O S

Kainos Publishing is an imprint of Supernatural Truth Productions, LLC.
KainosPublishing.com

Copyright © 2024, Art Thomas

Unless otherwise indicated, all Scripture quotations are taken from the Holy Bible, New International Version®, NIV®. Copyright © 1973, 1978, 1984, 2011 by Biblica, Inc.™ Used by permission of Zondervan. All rights reserved worldwide. www.zondervan.com The "NIV" and "New International Version" are trademarks registered in the United States Patent and Trademark Office by Biblica, Inc.™

All Scripture quotations marked (NKJV) are taken from the New King James Version®. Copyright © 1982 by Thomas Nelson. Used by permission. All rights reserved.

All Scripture quotations marked (MEV) are taken from the Modern English Version. Copyright © 2014 by Military Bible Association. Used by permission. All rights reserved.

All testimonies in this book are true and used with permission and approval of those they reference. Some of the names have been changed for privacy reasons, and some details have been omitted, inserted, or emphasized for the sake of maintaining focus on the intended point or lesson being taught.

In an effort to glorify God with honest and accurate testimonies that give hope and build faith, occasional mature themes are mentioned, such as abuse, infidelity, and violence. Also, since this is a book about marriage, sexuality is discussed frankly but in an honorable way. Readers should be aware and proceed accordingly.

ISBN: 978-1-959547-05-1

Library of Congress Control Number:
2024941130

Library of Congress Cataloging-in-Publication Data
Names: Thomas, Arthur Randall, 1984– author
Title: Good News for Your Marriage: A Gospel-Centered Guide to a Victorious Marriage
Description: Romulus, Michigan : Kainos Publishing, 2024.
Identifiers: LCCN 2024941130 | ISBN 978-1-959547-05-1
Subjects: LCSH: Christian Marriage

For my wife:
Happy Fifteenth Anniversary

And for my wife's parents:
After forty-three years of marriage, you continue
to model what love and self-sacrifice look like,
both for each other and your family.
Also, you raised a good one.

And for my parents:
After sixty-two years of marriage,
you are showing the rest of us how it's done.
Mom and Dad, thank you for sowing into me
so that I can share Jesus around the world.
This book is another piece of your legacy.

Endorsements

There is nothing that exhibits and illustrates Christ's love for his church like marriage. God intends this union to be divinely blissful, eternally fruitful, and utterly fulfilling. No wonder it is under such attack in our time, and never before have we so deeply needed wise and biblical encouragement in our marriages.

This is why I highly recommend Art Thomas's book *Good News for Your Marriage*. Art's unique perspective is gospel-centered and Spirit-led. And it's written by a man who, together with his wife, Robin, provides a shining example of what marriage can and should be.

Daniel Kolenda
President, Christ for All Nations
Lead Pastor, Nations Church, Orlando, FL
cfan.org | WeAreNations.church

The importance of cultivating a healthy marriage cannot be underestimated. Through theological principles and practical concepts, Art does a masterful job of teaching what a healthy Christian marriage looks like. This book would be an excellent tool to help strengthen marriages in your local church.

Aaron Hlavin
Network Superintendent
Assemblies of God, Michigan Ministry Network
mmn.ag

If you desire healing in your soul, mind, and marriage, then Art Thomas's book will help you. Art's writings reflect the heart of a man who desires to honor Jesus Christ and to love his wife the same way Christ loves his church.

James Dignan, MSLLP
Clinical Psychologist, Masters Level
Abundant Life Christian Counseling, Livonia, MI
alcc.us

This is literally the best book I've ever read on the subject of Christ-centered marriage (no exaggeration!). *Good News for Your Marriage* is filled with faith and hope and drives home this desperately needed revelation: the strength of your marriage is not found in your spouse but in the Lord. (Mic drop!) While deeply spiritual, it is also intensely practical and would make a great study for couples in healthy and hurting marriages, as well as for pre-marital counseling. Art, you've knocked it out of the park once again!

Dr. Jamie Morgan, DMin
Founder and Director, Trailblazer Mentoring Network
TrailblazerMentoring.com

In both my own marriage and pastoral ministry for thirty-five years, I thought I'd seen it all when it comes to the subject of marriage. I've taught (and been taught) marriage at seminars, retreats, and congregations for decades. But as I turned the pages of this book, I found myself seeing ideas I'd never considered before. The insights in these pages were both ancient and groundbreaking and connected the dots in my own marriage in profound ways. I don't use the word *masterpiece* often, but this book is simply that—a masterpiece of theology, storytelling, and wisdom. I highly recommend you read and study this book with your spouse and a team of friends.

Jim Wiegand
Senior Pastor, Freedom Center Church, Fenton, MI
FreedomCenter.church

In this book, Art Thomas has beautifully knit the gospel message together with God's design for marriage. If you have been looking for a rare find on the biblical perspective of marriage, then this book is for you. When applied, Art's uncommon wisdom and insightful perspective will captivate the reader and bring miraculous transformation to your relationship. Pick it up, read it, and put it to use!

Tim Bridgewater, MA and
Debbie Bridgewater, MA
Shilo Guidance Center, Boise, ID
ShiloCenter.com

Regardless of your marital state—single, desiring marriage, married, or single again—you will find value in this book. Art speaks to the foundation of marriage in Christ and the redemption our Lord offers everyone.

The pursuit of marriage is good; the pursuit of a healthy and holy marriage is incredible. Having a marriage founded in Christ is among the greatest treasures to behold.

Art provides wisdom from both experience and study that will encourage and challenge you to find everything God has for you, whatever your stage in life. The Lord can bring healing, joy, and newness to any marriage but also to each spouse. Above all, God redeems and writes a better story than we could write ourselves.

Mandy Crispin, MA
Ordained minister
Assemblies of God, Potomac Ministry Network

Good news! Art Thomas has given us a gift in *Good News for Your Marriage*. This immensely practical theology of marriage invites us to lean into God's design and experience all the goodness he has for us.

Josh Spurlock, MA, LPC, CST
Pastor, Licensed Counselor, and Sex Therapist
Founder of MyCounselor.Online
JoshSpurlock.com

God set marriage in the earth to be a living example of the power of unity and agreement. He designed marriage to be a demonstration of his love, faith, and commitment. According to Ephesians, marriage gives us a better understanding of the relationship between Christ and the church.

I am excited to recommend Art Thomas's book, *Good News for Your Marriage*. It is biblically based and full of godly wisdom. Any married couple or anyone hoping to be married will be enriched, enlightened, and grounded in present truth concerning God's will for marriage.

Bishop Victor L. Hill
Senior Pastor, Providence Christian Ministries, Birmingham, AL
pcmLive.org

Good News for Your Marriage ~ Art Thomas

Good News for Your Marriage provides valuable insight on growing and maintaining your marriage from both a spiritual and therapeutic perspective. As a counselor, I would highly recommend this book to Christian couples who are wanting to improve their marriage and examine how their marriage can lead others to the good news of Christ.

Liz Jans, MEd, LPC
Licensed Professional Counselor, Ordained Minister
Owner of Jans Counseling Services, Colorado Springs, CO

The revelation Art shares in this book breathes fresh life into marriages. It not only gives proper motivation and weight as to why marriage matters for the kingdom but also shows readers how to practically walk the path that leads to a radiant, passion-filled union that embodies Christ and the church. In *Good News for Your Marriage,* both husbands and wives will find freedom, refreshing, and hope for their marriages as they open their hearts to God.

Heather Carlisle
Founder of The Sanctuary Coaching and
The Come Away Retreat
TheSanctuaryCoaching.com

Contents

Foreword

ART AND I MET WHEN I WAS FIFTEEN AND HE WAS SEVENTEEN. People are often surprised when they hear we dated for seven years, but I like to joke that part of that was high school dating and doesn't really count.

When we got married, I thought I had life all figured out. Now, as my twentieth high school reunion approaches—after seven years of dating and fifteen years of marriage—I see just how little I knew at the time. While I'm sure we'll always be learning, this book contains the life-changing revelations Art and I have received regarding our marriage.

My prayer is that while you read this book, your heart remains teachable and sensitive to the Holy Spirit. I was not always responsive to the Lord in this way. During our dating years, Art and I had our share of fights and arguments. One was bad enough that I broke up with him. The breakup lasted about a week before we reconciled. By the time we were married, I figured that we had done all our major fighting during our seven years of dating, and I expected our marriage to begin with a bit of a head start because of that. I was surprised and frustrated by the fact that we still had newlywed arguments and problems.

At that point in our relationship, I believed that I was emotionally heathy and stable and all the problems we were having were because Art needed to grow and become more like Jesus. Of course, I now know this was prideful and sinful. The Lord had to work on my heart to get me to see that I needed to grow and become more like Jesus as well.

If you are reading this book and you are not ready for the Lord to do a work in your heart, my prayer is that you humble yourself before the Lord and consider these words from a perspective of allowing yourself to be molded more and more into the image of God. First, ask the Lord to take the plank out of your own eye before trying to remove the speck from your spouse's eye (Matthew 7:3–5).

Art and I have conducted pre-marital counseling with several couples over the years. One thing that we always tell them, even though it doesn't sound particularly romantic, is that we do not believe there is one special person out there for each person. We like to say that "the one" is the one you marry. If life circumstances had been different and I had never met Art, I believe that we could each have found someone else to be happy with. I don't love and devote myself to Art because I am destined to be with him. I wake up every morning and *choose* to love him and devote myself to him. I made a vow before God that I would love him "for better or for worse," and I am standing by that, no matter what life throws at us. By starting from a foundation of choosing to commit to one another, our marriage has now bloomed into one of deep emotional connection and friendship.

Finding "the one" you are meant to spend the rest of your life with makes a nice Hallmark movie, but it's just not real life. The Bible does not command us to marry "the one" or even to marry someone we are in love with. The Bible, which was largely written to cultures where arranged marriages were common, simply commands us to love the person we are married to.

What does that mean? Jesus told his disciples, "Greater love has no one than this: to lay down one's life for one's friends" (John 15:13). Jesus defined love as self-sacrifice and then demonstrated that self-sacrifice when he laid down his life for us at the cross.

Art and I have found a rhythm of life that consists of me putting his needs first and him putting my needs first. This includes little sacrifices like offering him the last cookie on a plate (even though I'd like it too) all the way to staying home with our two boys when they were little (and very active) while he followed God's call to evangelize and preach around the world. Meanwhile,

Art would stay home with the boys during the summer, while I worked at my family's seasonal business.

Finding this balance was difficult at first, and I had to figure out how to support his calling. But when our boys were two and four, I was supposed to attend a week-long out-of-state training for my summer job. Art didn't hesitate when I told him about it. "Of course, I'll stay home alone with the boys this time while you travel." Then, when my mom guilt was getting to me, he sent me videos of him and the boys playing and told me how proud he was of me.

Whenever I stayed home with the kids and Art traveled, my attitude was not "he's really going to owe me for this." I was not keeping track of how many days and weeks it had been my turn as the only parent home. I was truly acting out of love and keeping no record of it. Then, when he selflessly offered to do the same for me without hesitation, I didn't feel like I was collecting a debt that was owed to me. Instead, I simply felt truly loved and cared for. First Corinthians 13:5 says that love "keeps no record of wrongs," but I would like to add that love also keeps no record of how many "rights" you have done for your spouse. Everything is done out of self-sacrificial love.

This book may challenge your concept of marriage. You may find, like I did, that you are wrong in some areas that you did not recognize before. I truly believe that this book points you toward the true model of a healthy marriage that God intended. This is not a manual on "how to fix my spouse." If you are reading this book, it's because you sincerely want your marriage to be everything that God intends it to be. This is what we have witnessed in our own marriage and in so many marriages we've had the privilege of helping over the years. I expect this message to breathe life into your marriage as well. May God bless you as you read, and may God bless your marriage.

Preface

YES, YOU NEED TO READ THIS PREFACE.

If you're anything like me, you might skip over the preface in most books, but this time, I'm putting the most important and life-changing information right here at the start. Everything that follows hinges on this.

This book is called *Good News for Your Marriage* because it is an application of the best news in the universe, specifically in the context of your relationship with your spouse. But before that good news will be particularly helpful to your marriage, it needs to be internalized. You have to know it personally before you can know it together.

You may be thinking, *I already know the gospel.* I hope that's true. But my travels around the world have proven to me that far too many Christians don't realize the glory and magnitude of what Jesus has done for them. I've even had pastors respond publicly, in front of their congregations, to an invitation to receive salvation for the first time—not because my preaching was amazing but because they realized they had somehow managed to attain their position without truly bowing to King Jesus.

I grew up in a Christian home with wonderful, godly parents. But even the best parents in the world can't protect you from everything. When I was about seven or eight years old, I was sexually abused by some older boys in my neighborhood. It didn't take long before I went from victim to participant, playing along with the so-called game.

A couple of years later, a friend down the street introduced me to a pornographic magazine that he found under his dad's mattress. Soon, I was addicted, and the struggle followed me well into my teen years.

The worst part, it seemed, was that I still really loved Jesus. I desperately wanted to be free. But I also believed I was the only person struggling with these issues and assumed no one else would understand. I was tricked into isolation, trying desperately to find freedom in my own strength but failing at every turn.

Sin thrives in isolation. And part of our struggle to overcome sin is that it's not well defined in our culture. Sin is not a list of bad behaviors that we're supposed to avoid. Sin is anything that misses the target of living according to God's original design for us, which is to be expressions of his image and likeness (Genesis 1:26–27). To sin is to fall short of God's glory—in other words, to fail to reveal God's nature through our attitudes, actions, words, and lifestyles (Romans 3:23).

Jesus is both God and the Son of God (John 1:1). He came to earth as a human being, born as a helpless baby to a poor family (Philippians 2:6–8). He lived a perfectly sinless life—not in his own strength but completely depending on Father God (John 5:19; Hebrews 4:15). He worked so many miracles and showed so much love and compassion that all the books in the world could not contain the record of his works (John 21:25).

Nevertheless, Jesus was arrested, brutalized, and murdered on a cross, dying a criminal's death. Then, on the morning of the third day after his death, Jesus rose from the dead, victorious.

That's the part we basically all know. Countless Christians around the world are satisfied with this much of the gospel, rejoicing in God's forgiveness and now aiming to honor him with their whole lives as they look forward to an eternity with him. We thank God for the blood of Jesus, which procures forgiveness for us. And we celebrate his resurrection from the dead, which proves that he conquered sin and death for us. This is where most people are offered an opportunity to respond to the gospel and receive salvation. But the gospel doesn't stop there.

My personal testimony includes more than what I've shared here, and I'll spare you the longer version in this context. But the revelation that transformed my life when I was sixteen is that

God's forgiveness wasn't all I needed. There's much more to our salvation. Forgiveness was available under the Old Testament system of laws and sacrifices. If forgiveness were all that is needed for a Christian life, then Jesus didn't need to come.

The Bible says that Jesus took all our sin into his body on the cross, to such a degree that he became sin personified (1 Peter 2:24; 2 Corinthians 5:21). Accordingly, when Jesus died, all our sinful brokenness died with him (Romans 8:3). Because Jesus died, everything about our old way of living can also be considered dead (Romans 6:11). Everything about us that doesn't measure up to who God is or who he designed us to be is now defeated. And when we trust him and his work, we receive all the benefits of his victory, making us into completely new people.

Throughout my years of sin, addiction, emotional outbursts, bitterness, lust, sensuality, and negative attitudes, I came to Jesus again and again to be forgiven, but I had never come to him to die.

The apostle Paul wrote, "I have been crucified with Christ and I no longer live, but Christ lives in me. The life I now live in the body, I live by faith in the Son of God, who loved me and gave himself for me" (Galatians 2:20). When we believe the good news that what Jesus accomplished for us is enough to rescue us from our broken lifestyles, personal transformation follows.

Remember, Jesus didn't only die; he rose from the dead. When you partnered with him in his death (by surrendering your old life and agreeing that there's nothing you can add to his work on the cross to make you any more saved or free), the natural outcome is that you also partner with him in his resurrection (Romans 6:5). Accordingly, the same Spirit of God who raised Jesus from the dead comes to live inside you as a down payment of resurrection life, guaranteeing your eternal future with the Lord (Romans 8:11; 2 Corinthians 1:21–22; Ephesians 1:13–14).

And yet, the good news continues and becomes even better. In Ephesians 2:6, Paul wrote that "God raised us up with Christ and seated us with him in the heavenly realms in Christ Jesus." In other words, we've been invited to live victoriously in union with Jesus—not as he was two thousand years ago but as he is today, risen and exalted at the right hand of Father God in heaven (1 John 4:17). He shares his authority with us. He shares his victory with us. And, most importantly, he shares with us his union and intimacy with Father God.

When we put our faith in Jesus, he puts his Holy Spirit into our bodies, and we become living, breathing temples for God to dwell within—brand-new people, united with God (1 Corinthians 6:15–20). As Paul explained, "Therefore, if anyone is in Christ, the new creation has come: The old has gone, the new is here!" (2 Corinthians 5:17).

There are two spiritual kingdoms: the kingdom of light and the kingdom of darkness. The kingdom of light consists of everything good, perfect, pure, beautiful, and life-giving. Meanwhile, the kingdom of darkness contains imperfect shadows and perversions of those virtues, each skewed by pain, brokenness, chaos, evil, deception, manipulation, and death.

The ruler of the kingdom of light is Jesus Christ. Meanwhile, the kingdom of darkness is in turmoil, and an evil spirit called Satan exerts influence there, trying to keep people blind to God's superior kingdom (2 Corinthians 4:4).

The kingdom of darkness has been the default influence in this world ever since the first humans sinned. But Jesus decided to bring the light of his kingdom into our world, showing us what it looks like when a human being lives free from sin, in right relationship with Father God. He brought order to the chaos. He forgave sin. He fed the hungry, healed the sick, raised the dead, and drove out demons.

Regarding Jesus, John wrote, "The light shines in the darkness, and the darkness has not overcome it" (John 1:5). Everywhere Jesus went, he shined the light of his Father's kingdom. And most importantly, he made a way to rescue us out of the kingdom of darkness and unite us with himself, turning us into people of light as well. Ephesians 5:8 tells us that we Christians were once darkness, but now we too are light.

That's what the cross and resurrection are really about—becoming who Jesus is.

It's easy to be part of the kingdom of darkness. All you have to do is live in your own strength, never truly depending on God. Unfortunately, a lot of Christians live this way. Perhaps you do. Even if you've called out to Jesus for your salvation, if you're not relying on his Spirit to produce new life in you, then you're still wallowing in darkness.

You might even be a decent person. Perhaps you were raised well and have no real vices to overcome. But when we admit that even our greatest virtues are still darkness compared to the perfection Jesus displays, we can then call out to Jesus for help. We can die to our old self-sufficient ways of living and embrace a new way of being united with the King of light. Suddenly, his light shines through us, and we find ourselves doing the same things Jesus did when he walked this earth, and greater (John 14:12).

And that's *my* story. I'm a new creation. I've been free from that addiction to pornography and perversion for about two decades, and now my life is marked with supernatural love, extravagant generosity, miracle-working power, and the victory of Jesus. I can say boldly that our God is mighty to save. Step by step, my life has been transformed to look more and more like Jesus. I have a considerable distance to go before I perfectly reveal him in every way, but I'm more like him today than I've ever been.

Perhaps you have been thoughtfully considering the gospel as you read my story and these explanations. Perhaps you recognize that you have been living according to your own strength, not yet surrendering fully to Jesus. It's time to be transformed from darkness to light.

I like to describe Christian conversion as though you are signing your name to the bottom of a blank contract, handing it to Jesus, and saying, "You fill in the details. I don't care what it costs me—I see now that you're worth any cost. I'm surrendering my definition of morality, my ideas about who I am, and my hopes and dreams for the future. And I submit to your definition of morality, your ideas about who I am, and your hopes and dreams for my future. You can keep adding details to that contract for the rest of my life, and I will always say 'yes' because you are Lord, and I trust you. I know you love me, and I believe that no matter what you tell me to do in life, I can trust you to live through me to accomplish it."

My personal experience and that of untold millions of other people throughout history is that when you give all of your life to Jesus like that, he gives you all of his life by putting his Holy Spirit inside you and transforming you into a new creation—someone who never existed before. This is the Christian life.

We can't do this in our own strength. It's moment-by-moment dependence on God's strength and power. It's daily surrender to God's will and ability, trusting that he will express himself through you as you remain in an attitude of simple faith.

If you've never surrendered your life to Jesus like this, the way into this lifestyle is simple. Romans 10:9 says, "If you declare with your mouth, 'Jesus is Lord,' and believe in your heart that God raised him from the dead, you will be saved." I assume you believe Jesus rose from the dead if you're responding to the message I've shared here. That only leaves one more requirement: an action of your will that is akin to signing that blank contract. Speak out loud your allegiance to the King of the kingdom of light. Simply declare, "Jesus, you are Lord."

If you've just done this, I bless you in the name of Jesus and pray your life will never be the same. You are forgiven of all your sin—everything you have ever said, thought, or done that falls short of God's perfection and design for your life. I command every spirit of darkness to let you go in the name of Jesus. Be free. And right now, receive the Holy Spirit. Be made new.

Welcome to my family! If you're not yet part of a church, I recommend you find one as soon as possible.[1] Ask to be baptized in water because this is the first act of obedience to Jesus that is expected of a new disciple. Your immersion in water and reemergence is a prophetic picture of your old life dying and going into the grave, followed by your new life raising up in the power of God. It's a thrilling experience, and necessary, so don't put it off.

Okay. *Now* we're ready to talk about your marriage.

---

[1] Not every church is a great church, and you may need to check out several in your area before you feel like you've found the right spiritual family. Look for a church that is grounded in the Scriptures, full of the Holy Spirit, supporting missionaries, leading people to Jesus, and bursting with love for each other. Every church has its strengths and weaknesses. If you have a Christian friend you admire, their church is probably the best place to start.

Acknowledgments

Naturally, I'm grateful for Jesus and my amazing wife, Robin. Without either, this book could have never been written. Every page is a tribute to both and an expression of the many lessons I've learned in union with them.

I have been blessed by many godly examples of healthy marriages, including both Robin's and my parents, plus so many pastors and leaders in our lives—especially Dan and Sarita Vander Velde and Brooks and Tammy McElhenny.

I want to offer a special thanks to Pastor Bruce and Linda Stefanik at Church on the Hill in Salem, Oregon. I wrote nearly half of this book while staying in their guest room in October 2023. Bruce and Linda's commitment to a Christ-centered marriage and their emphasis on cultivating healthy marriages in their church created a spiritual environment of peace and revelation for this book to take shape. Their passion for the gospel, commitment to the mission, and love for Jesus and his bride are contagious. I'm grateful for their example to the body of Christ, their hospitality, and their insistence on taking me out for an amazing cheesecake.

I also want to offer a special thanks to the many pastors, psychologists, counselors, theologians, therapists, and beta readers who helped hone this book's message before it went to print, and to my editor, Lisa Thompson, for her Spirit-filled attention to detail and excellent insights. This book's effectiveness is the fruit of your labor.

First Things First

EVERY BIT OF ADVICE IN THIS BOOK ASSUMES THAT YOU AND your spouse are both safe. If you are in an abusive situation, get out. Find safety. *Then* read this book. You are under no obligation to subject yourself or your children to danger of any kind. Talk to your pastor about finding the help you need.

Not all abuse is physical; abuse can also be emotional, spiritual, sexual, financial, and more. If you're in an emotionally abusive situation, you may need to separate from your spouse for a time until they are repentant and you feel stable and ready to enforce healthy boundaries. We'll talk about how to exercise boundaries later in this book. We'll also talk about times when divorce may be called for.

If you aren't sure if your situation is abusive, talk to trusted friends, pastors, or a licensed Christian counselor to determine if you need to exercise space in your current relationship. You don't have to figure it all out alone.

Also, in today's world, I need to state that I am writing this book for a Christian audience who subscribes to the biblical definition of a marriage, which is a covenant (a promise blessed by God that only ends through death) between one biological man and one biological woman. While other types of couples are welcome to read this book, such readers ought to understand that the advice offered fits a specific context that they're invited into, not their current lifestyle. Nevertheless, no matter who you are or what your beliefs are on this topic, I do believe that reading this book will point you to Jesus and help you find wholeness in him as he liberates you from sin and its effects.

Good News for Your Marriage ~ Art Thomas

Every marriage is different, but Jesus remains the same. The gospel works in every context. If any solution I suggest doesn't quite fit your specific situation, talk to your spouse about how to apply the broader gospel principle. There is hope for every marriage where Christ has been welcomed, and it is found in the gospel of Jesus Christ.

Introduction

YOUR MARRIAGE MATTERS TO GOD. IF YOU'RE READING THIS book alone and wishing your spouse were reading too, don't worry. Someone far greater than your spouse wants your marriage to thrive even more than you do. Our Lord is on your team and will gladly partner with anyone who stands in faith for a successful marriage. And if you're reading this book along with your spouse, even better.

I do not write to fix you or your spouse, but if you will embrace the message of this book, it will indeed transform your life for the better. That's because the core message of this book is the gospel—the good news of King Jesus and what he has accomplished for you—and that gospel is powerful to transform both of you into the people you were always created to be.

Every couple is unique, but the gospel is always effective. Perhaps your relationship is already healthy. If so, the gospel will bring you even closer together while also making you into multipliers of God's kingdom, ministering to each other and the world with God's power and love. Perhaps your relationship is chaotic. If so, the gospel will bring you to a real experience of peace from the Lord. Perhaps your relationship is distant. If so, the gospel will teach you to love and receive love. And even if your marriage feels like it's hanging on by a thread or like all hope is already lost, let me remind you that the gospel we received is about resurrection from the dead. No couple is too far gone when the gospel is at work to transform the lives of a husband and wife.

Good News for Your Marriage ~ Art Thomas

I've seen a couple with divorce papers in hand choose faith and thrive. I've seen a couple where the husband was sleeping in his truck in the garage experience Jesus and embrace a Spirit-filled life of love. I've seen a couple sleeping in separate rooms and considering divorce receive the gospel and become a healthy family again.

No matter what you're going through, let me give you some hope—not hope in this book, *per se*, but hope in the gospel I will present here. This is the gospel that transformed my life. And as my wife and I allowed the Holy Spirit to apply this gospel within our marriage, it transformed our relationship too.

Today, my wife and I are best friends, but that wasn't always the case. Robin and I met as teenagers when my family moved to a new church. We became an item about five months later. I was seventeen, and she was fifteen. I was head-over-heels in love, and she was, I think, cautiously optimistic.

We both had significant emotional struggles and sin issues. When we first got together, I was secretly addicted to pornography. In conflict, I would blame or shame her, or if that didn't work, I'd throw temper tantrums and fits of rage. I had a deep inner need to be perfect and never show any flaws, which led to emotional meltdowns, unreasonable blame shifting, and years of clinical depression.

Meanwhile, Robin had her own inner wounds. When her fight-or-flight response activated, she was all flight. If we were arguing on the phone, she would hang up on me (and I refused to chase her). She had her own insecurities from hurtful experiences growing up. Even though she came from a wonderful family, a variety of hurts throughout life had stacked up to make her emotionally fragile and easily triggered by my various antics.

But I was also a hopeless romantic, and somehow my steady outpouring of love notes, flowers, homemade love songs, and, I'm sure, stunning good looks managed to keep her coming back.

At one point, when I was working for her dad, he and I had a sharp disagreement when I thought he had fired me. Robin ran again. She broke up with me, saying, "If you can't get along with my dad, I don't know how we can be together." Our relationship was over for a week until we saw each other again and both agreed that it was the worst week of our lives. We were a complicated mess together but were happier together than apart. We also both genuinely loved Jesus, which gave us a solid common ground on which to stand.

A couple of years into our season of dating, when I was nineteen, God set me free from that addiction to pornography. Little by little, God worked on my heart, and little by little, Robin welcomed the same.

Robin's parents did not want her to get married until she graduated from college, and we decided to honor that request. Then Robin chose a double major and took five years to graduate. In all, that meant we dated seven years before being married on June 7, 2009.

It was probably just as well, though. We needed that time to sort through the worst of our personal struggles. By the time we were standing at the altar on our wedding day, we both thought we had overcome all our issues and could now live happily ever after.

Then reality set in. Suddenly, we were together in the same house with shared bills and responsibilities. The fairy tale quickly dissolved into a hurricane of frustrations, annoyances, and bickering. Both of us reverted to some of our old defense mechanisms. Barely two months into our marriage, Robin suggested divorce.

Fast-forward a couple of years into our marriage, and Robin and I would describe each other as best friends. We rarely fought. Our home became a place where we could drop our emotional walls and feel relaxed and free. And this feeling has never left.

At the time of this writing, Robin and I have been together twenty-two years, nearly fifteen of them married. For well over a decade, this has been the greatest marriage I can imagine, and Robin and I are more in love today than ever before. We have two rambunctious, creative, and hilarious boys who love the Lord and each other. Our home is a place of peace, joy, fun, and mutual affection.

Robin and I still have disagreements, but we work through them with gentleness and respect—not with forced behavior but a genuine honor and love for one another. We would rather spend time with each other than anyone else. We make disciples for Jesus in our home and have seen countless miracles and lives transformed in our living room. We both feel secure, healthy, and overflowing with hope for other married couples, no matter how messy their current situation.

What happened? What took place during those two years I just fast-forwarded over? What experiences and revelations transformed us and our relationship so thoroughly?

In short, God did a lot. For the long answer, keep reading. This book contains the gospel-born discoveries that were key in bringing us to the healthy place we are today. And we have seen these principles save multiple marriages over the years.

Every couple is different, and how you and your spouse implement these discoveries will likely vary. But I believe the gospel is so powerful and Jesus is so personal that what we share will breathe fresh life into your unique marriage.

You and your spouse can truly be each other's best friends. No matter where you are on your marital journey, I believe you are going to be a healthier person with more love to give by the time you finish reading.

I bless your marriage in the name of Jesus and pray that you and your spouse will be transformed for the better. No matter how messy life might seem right now, there really is good news for your marriage.

CHAPTER 1:

You Already Have a Perfect Marriage

"MAYBE WE SHOULD JUST GET A DIVORCE."
Robin stood on the opposite side of our bed, emotionally spent by our relentless arguing. Her defeated words stung every cell of my body.

Our relationship was terribly dysfunctional, but I had enough sense to recognize that our marriage covenant before God was sacred.

The term *covenant* is used 284 times in the Old Testament.[2] It's more than a mere promise. It's an earnest commitment with clearly defined guarantees and obligations attached.[3] That means a covenant implies the need for intentional effort to keep the terms of the contract. It's not a passive agreement that can be made and then ignored by one or both parties. In the Bible, the word is often used to describe a treaty, pact, or other formal agreement, not only between God and his people but also between any two individuals, political leaders, or states.[4] And in Malachi 2:14, the word is used in reference to marriage. Marriage, therefore, is a sacred responsibility

---

[2] "Lexicon :: Strong's H1285 – בְּרִית / bᵊrîṯ," Blue Letter Bible, accessed April 16, 2024, https://www.blueletterbible.org/lexicon/h1285/niv/wlc/0-1/.

[3] P. R. Williamson, "Covenant," *Dictionary of the Old Testament Pentateuch: A Compendium of Contemporary Biblical Scholarship*," eds. T. Desmond Alexander and David W. Baker (Downers Grove, Illinois: InterVarsity Press, 2003), 139.

[4] Denis Baley, BA, "Covenant," *Harper's Bible Dictionary*, gen. ed. Paul J. Achtemeier (San Francisco: HarperSanFrancisco, 1985), 190.

to someone—a pledge of commitment and union that is not to be neglected or treated lightly. It takes intentional effort to maintain. And as Robin spoke those stinging words, I refused to give up on such a God-given responsibility, simply because my new bride and I were overwhelmed with each other.

I came to my senses and said with conviction, "Do not ever say that word again. Divorce is not an option for us. We're struggling right now, but we're only going to get through this if we both know there's no turning back. We made a commitment before God to love, honor, and cherish each other, and I'm not about to throw that away just because we're being immature right now. We'll get through this."

I walked around the bed to Robin, and she melted into my arms. We cried together.

"I don't really want a divorce," she confessed.

"Me either, honey. We'll figure this out."

Your Marriage Is Stronger than Your Relationship

Robin and I had only been married a couple of months when that exchange took place, although we had dated for seven years. Our relationship was deeply flawed—infested with our sinful expressions of emotional wounds and selfish tendencies that had followed us from childhood. We were new at the whole marriage thing. But thankfully, the strength of our marriage was found in God's power and not our own.

Marriage is more about what God has done than anything we have done. The wedding ceremony comes with beautiful and important vows and promises, but all these vows and promises would be worthless if God did not join a couple together.

Whether or not it was voiced at your wedding ceremony, every marriage comes with a biblical blessing, spoken by the Lord Jesus himself: "'For this reason a man will leave his father and mother and be united to his wife, and the two will become one flesh.' So they are no longer two, but one flesh. *Therefore what God has joined together, let no one separate*" (Mark 10:7–9, emphasis added). You and your spouse are joined together, not by your promises, your character, your feelings, or your resolve, but by Almighty God.

Your marriage is not defined by your behaviors or those of your spouse. Your marriage is a work of God. It is a perfect covenant, blessed by the perfect Creator and Judge of all— bestowed upon you and your spouse to steward and enjoy to the fullest.

When people say things like, "My marriage is falling apart," or "I wish we had a better marriage," they indicate that they are defining their marriage more by their imperfect interactions than by the covenant itself. Your marriage isn't the problem; your experience of it is. Your perfect, God-given marriage is being eclipsed by sin, selfishness, and personal striving, believing the lie that your marriage is only as good as how the other person makes you feel.

If we think of your marriage as the rope that stretches between the two of you to bind you together in holy matrimony, then we can say that you have immediate access to the rope, even if your spouse is distant. The rope is good and perfect, even if you and your spouse are not. Either or both of you can lay hold of your good and perfect marriage right now, resting in the security of what God has already done.

In other words, you can enjoy a perfect marriage even before you or your spouse changes. Until we believe that our marriage is a good, God-given blessing, we will assume that our marriage is the problem. Accordingly, we'll focus all our attention on fixing our marriage rather than applying the gospel to our lives. We don't have marriage problems; we have sin problems. The first place to look for solutions is not in how to be set free from your marriage but in how to be set free from sin.

You Already Have Everything You Need

As a follower of Jesus, you already have everything you need to see your marriage thrive. In fact, as a follower of Jesus, you're already the person you need to be. The more clearly you can see this truth, the more you will live by faith and the less confidence you will put in your own ability.

Notice what the apostle Peter wrote: "His divine power has given us everything we need for a godly life through our knowledge of him who called us by his own glory and goodness" (2 Peter 1:3). Did you catch that? Because you know Jesus, God's power has *already* given you everything you need to live a godly life. You don't need more love for your spouse. You don't need more patience. You don't need more self-control. You already have everything you need.

You might ask, "Then why am I struggling to love my spouse? Why do I snap so quickly? Why can't I seem to behave kindly around them?"

It's simple. You're living in your flesh instead of trusting the Holy Spirit to express Jesus's life through you.

I'll admit, I don't like that answer. But that doesn't make it less true. Notice what the apostle Paul said about the difference between our flesh and life in the Spirit:

> If you bite and devour each other, watch out or you will be destroyed by each other.
>
> So I say, walk by the Spirit, and you will not gratify the desires of the flesh. For the flesh desires what is contrary to the Spirit, and the Spirit what is contrary to the flesh. They are in conflict with each other, so that you are not to do whatever you want. But if you are led by the Spirit, you are not under the law.
>
> The acts of the flesh are obvious: sexual immorality, impurity and debauchery; idolatry and witchcraft; hatred, discord, jealousy, fits of rage, selfish ambition, dissensions, factions and envy; drunkenness, orgies, and the like. I warn you, as I did before, that those who live like this will not inherit the kingdom of God.
>
> But the fruit of the Spirit is love, joy, peace, forbearance, kindness, goodness, faithfulness, gentleness and self-control. Against such things there is no law. Those who belong to Christ Jesus have crucified the flesh with its passions and desires. Since we live by the Spirit, let us keep in step with the Spirit. (Galatians 5:15–25)

Notice that the Scriptures offer us a distinction between "the acts of the flesh" and "the fruit of the Spirit." There's a difference between *acts* and *fruit*. Acts happen through our strength, but fruit happens through our identity.

Pardon the crude analogy, but I've never seen a constipated tree, wincing and striving to squeeze out some fruit. All a tree has to do to produce good fruit is be rooted in good soil and receive sunshine and water from God. If you're rooted in God's love, receiving nourishment for your soul from him, then you have everything you need.

Also, notice that the *acts* are plural while the *fruit* is singular. The virtues Paul listed are not multiple fruits; they're all one fruit of the Spirit. If you have the Spirit, then you have the whole fruit.

Remember, you already have everything you need for a godly life because you know Jesus. In other words, you already have all the love you will ever need. When you let yourself be loved by him, his love overflows out of your life (1 John 4:19). If you're struggling to love your spouse, it's only because you're not yet internalizing God's love, which is already given to you.

This is usually because we believe lies about ourselves—that we are unlovable. Or we might believe lies about God—that he is unloving. But when we look at the proof Jesus offered us through his life, death, and resurrection—when we honor the Scriptures above our experiences—those lies make their way to the cross, and a cascade of heavenly love pours into our hearts.

Similarly, you don't need more patience. We often think of patience as numbness to the waiting process or aloofness to daily annoyances. This is why the Bible translation quoted above uses the word *forbearance* where other translations might use *patience*. Still others use *longsuffering*. Real patience is the strength to endure. If you tell yourself that you don't have patience, then you will give yourself excuses for buckling under the stresses of life. But if you believe the truth that God's divine power has already given you all the patience you will ever need, then you can trust the Holy Spirit who lives in you to empower you through any trial.

The same goes for self-control. This is not a skill that you develop over time. It's not a virtue that belongs only to the super-mature. It is part of the fruit of the Holy Spirit—the one fruit that you already possess because God lives in you. He has all the self-control you will ever need, and he can express it through you when you believe he's already there to give you victory.

It's Not Your Fruit

It's in your nature as a new creation in Christ to produce Jesus's fruit. In John 15:5, Jesus said, "I am the vine; you are the branches. If you remain in me and I in you, you will bear much fruit; apart from me you can do nothing."

Grapes are called the "fruit of the vine," not the "fruit of the branches." Branches disconnected from the vine produce nothing. But connected branches produce the vine's fruit. In the same way, when we are united to Jesus—considering our old, independent lives to be dead and trusting his Spirit who lives in us—suddenly, we find ourselves looking more and more like Jesus. This was always God's plan for you—to be "conformed to the image of his Son" (Romans 8:29).

Just after saying that God's power has given us everything we need for a godly life, Peter continued, stating that through God's glory and goodness, "he has given us his very great and precious promises, so that through them *you may participate in the divine nature*, having escaped the corruption in the world caused by evil desires" (2 Peter 1:4, emphasis added). God has spoken promises over you that if you will trust him, will enable you to participate in his nature.

Imagine what will happen as you embrace this truth and start revealing Jesus's nature to your spouse. It will probably go one of two ways. The only person who has ever been perfectly Christlike at all times and in every way—Christ—received two responses to his lifestyle. Either people were transformed in his presence, or they tried to kill him. I can't promise that if you start revealing Jesus to your spouse that everything will go perfectly according to plan. What I can promise is that this is what you were created for, and it's the only lifestyle worth living. Jesus is worthy of your whole life, no matter the cost. Eternal life is for those who persevere with uncompromising faith.

God's grace is not merely his act of saving us. God's grace is his empowering favor that enables us to live differently than would be possible on our own. His grace empowers us to say no to the sinful mindsets and lifestyles that our flesh prefers and yes to the Holy Spirit who lives in us (Titus 2:11–12). And if you want to live in the power of that grace, then you will need to choose a mindset of humility.

The Bible warns us that "God resists the proud, but gives grace to the humble" (James 4:6 NKJV). If you want God's empowering favor to rest on your life, then you need to admit your desperate need for him. God's power is only available to those who admit they need it and cry out for his help (2 Corinthians 12:9–10).

If you need Jesus to intervene in your relationship with your spouse, then you need to lead a lifestyle where he can live through you to exercise his will. Perhaps you have prayed in desperation for God to fix your spouse, waiting for their behavior to change before you can feel okay. Meanwhile, the very vessel God wants to use to show his transformative love to your spouse is frustrated and cowering, focusing more on how your spouse makes you feel than on how to reveal Jesus to them.

I know this because I've lived it. Our self-centered prayers can go on for years if we falsely believe that our personal well-being depends on our spouse's words and actions. If Jesus is your source, then your spouse can remain unchanged for the rest of your life, and you will nevertheless continue to reveal more and more of Jesus.

Your Marriage Is Stronger than Your Spouse

When we expect our marriage's strength to come from our spouse's behaviors and decisions rather than from God, we define our marriage as being only as good as the weakest partner. It's a broken, worldly distortion of a beautiful, holy reality. When we don't see the beautiful covenant God has created to bind the two of us together in his sight, we frantically grasp at each other, desperately wishing that the other person were stronger so that our marriage could be better.

Imagine if Jesus thought that way about his bride, the church. Imagine if Jesus used our imperfections as an excuse to be a jerk. Imagine if Jesus mocked us or berated us, saying it's our fault that he acts inappropriately. If that were true, then the gospel would be no gospel at all.

Thank God, Jesus's perfection does not depend on our perfection! Instead, he proactively loves, forgives, nurtures, and serves us despite all our imperfections and failures. His love helps us understand Father God and brings us transformation. And that same Jesus wants to live through you to minister to your spouse.

Your spouse doesn't need to be stronger than you; your marriage covenant is already stronger than you. If you will personally cling to the Lord and celebrate the covenant he has blessed to join you and your spouse, then you can lay hold of your perfect marriage today.

Furthermore, you don't need to be stronger than your spouse. If you think it's hard to express Jesus's nature to your spouse all day, every day, you're wrong. It's not hard; it's impossible. As long as you think it's hard, the only solution is to try harder. But that's exhausting and can never be accomplished. Once you see that it's truly impossible, the only solution is to die to your own effort and trust the Holy Spirit to produce Jesus's life through you.

None of us is strong enough, smart enough, kind enough, forgiving enough, wise enough, or spiritual enough to live as God created us to live. That's because God specifically designed us to need him. Apart from Jesus, we can do nothing (John 15:5). If you have been striving for a perfect marriage in your own strength, I want to set you free. It's not your responsibility to make your marriage perfect; God already did that. It's your responsibility—in the strength of the Lord—to selflessly love your imperfect spouse, surrendered to the Holy Spirit who lives in you.

You can have a wonderful marriage *right now*. Your spouse may be a challenge to live with. He or she may have all manner of annoying quirks, inner wounds, and emotional walls. Nevertheless, it is possible for you to personally engage in and enjoy many of the blessings of that perfect covenant, even if your spouse is not engaging in or enjoying the same. You can let your heart rest in the integrity of your supernatural bond. The covenant is no less valid or good simply because one spouse is failing to enjoy it.

You don't have to wait until you finish reading this book to enjoy a strong marriage. You already have it.

Gathering Your Thoughts

Write down your thoughts about these questions before talking to your spouse about this chapter. Talk to the Lord about any shortcomings you see in yourself, and simply trust him to immediately bring forgiveness, freedom, and transformation to your heart.

1. What are some virtues that are built into your character but are still inferior to Jesus's perfection? What needs to change in your heart so that you can produce Jesus's fruit instead of your own?
2. What are some sinful attitudes and actions you see in yourself that you have blamed on your spouse's behavior? What are some sinful attitudes and actions that you know are entirely your own issues?
3. What are some aspects of your relationship that you thought were *hard* (implying that you need to exert strength to overcome) instead of *impossible* (implying that you need God's power to overcome as you surrender to him)?

Conversation Starters

Open up to your spouse about the following topics. Require nothing from them—only give.

1. Share what impacted you most about this chapter.
2. Are you aware of anything you need to apologize for? If so, offer a heartfelt apology to your spouse.
3. What are some ways you have seen Jesus reveal himself through your spouse? Share your observations with them and encourage them.

Ask your spouse the following:

1. What are your favorite aspects of our relationship?

CHAPTER 2:

Rooted in God's Love

AT ONE O'CLOCK IN THE MORNING, I WOULD HAVE RATHER been sleeping than zipping down the expressway to break up a fight between a couple in my church who desperately needed intervention.

In the spring of 2018, I met a recent widower who lost his wife of nearly forty years to cancer. He began attending a weekly meeting I held in my home, which a year later would expand to become Roots Church. Ron was the son of a pastor and grew up knowing the Lord. He had been the head trustee of a church that closed when its pastor moved out of state. He was grieving his late wife but was also stable, grounded in the Word, and full of faith.

In preparation to officially organize our new church the following year, I asked Ron to serve on our senior leadership team as our executive director to help oversee all the legal and financial matters for the organization. He agreed, and we began planning.

That October, Ron met Connie—a vibrant, fun, and Spirit-filled woman. She had weathered some terrible relational situations in her past. Her third and most recent husband of sixteen years—a deacon and a youth minister with her in a large church—had abandoned her for a year while she prayed for God to save their marriage. Eventually, she learned that he was having an affair. The betrayal led to divorce, and Connie stayed single for four years before meeting Ron.

From the very start of their relationship, they saw that they had much in common—especially their desires to serve together in church and start a marriage ministry. I was overjoyed to see two mature believers who had both experienced so much heartache find each other. They were engaged the following April.

Around that time, Connie was diagnosed with Stage 4 ovarian cancer, leading to major surgery five weeks before the wedding. But Ron said he asked her to marry him, and he wasn't changing his mind. I performed their wedding that June.

But on the drive home from the wedding, all hell broke loose. Connie turned into a different person, lashing out in rage and vicious language. Ron almost cancelled the honeymoon, which turned out to be marked more with pain and anger than the joyful bonding experience it should have been.

After the honeymoon, Ron called to tell me what was happening. He said, "I know we're supposed to launch this church in August, but I'm afraid this is going to end in divorce. I don't want to drag you or the church through any of my mess, so I'm thinking I should step down and let someone else fill my position."

I replied, "Ron, I believe I was led by the Spirit when I chose you for this role, and I'm in this with you. As far as I can tell, you're still living righteously, so I'm not going to turn you away for your wife's behavior. If it blows up into a huge mess, then I'll walk through it with you. That's what family does. Thanks for telling me what's happening, but we're in this together, and I'm choosing you for my leadership team, mess and all."

In the ensuing months, Ron and Connie battled almost constantly. Their home was a warzone. Connie would scream at the top of her lungs and slam doors so hard, the trim would pull away from the wall. She would swear at him and call him names. She once kicked the bedroom door shut with such force that her foot put a hole in the door. Her outbursts of rage were out of control.

Ron was shellshocked. He'd be the first to tell you that he wasn't perfect in all his responses, but it was still clear as to who was the victim and who was damaging their house. I told Ron many times that he was not obligated to put himself in danger or subject himself to such behavior, but he assured me that the Lord was strengthening him and he wanted to be there for Connie. He knew she needed an encounter with Jesus, and he said that he didn't know who would give that to her if not him. Ron willingly returned to the battle day after day, knowing full well that he was not obligated to do so. He anchored himself in God's love and tried his best to overflow that same love to his wife.

I referred them to professional help while offering to be a friend and pastor. Multiple times a week, I had long conversations with Ron, helping him process his feelings, identify and repent of his own sinful responses, and choose love.

Connie seemed to want nothing to do with our church, so we couldn't exercise any sort of church discipline to help her come to her senses. She had already removed herself from fellowship, leaving Ron to attend alone most of the time.

Occasionally, I drove to their house for pastoral counseling and emergency help. And that's how I found myself racing down the expressway at one o'clock in the morning, not knowing what sort of scene I was about to walk in on.

What Are We Doing Here?

A friend of mine, J.P. Dorsey, once lamented to me that in all his years of talking with young couples before their weddings, when he has asked why they want to be married, he has never heard someone say, "Because I'm so satisfied and fulfilled in God's love that I have an abundance of love to give, and I decided this is the person I want to selflessly bless and serve for the rest of my life."

Instead, the answers are stereotypically romantic. "She's perfect for me." "He completes me." "I've never known anyone who makes me feel so loved and cherished." "There's no one I would rather spend my life with."

At the core of all these reasons is an emphasis on self and how the other person makes us feel.

But what happens when the other person inevitably makes us feel bad? What happens when someone else comes along who makes us feel better than our spouse makes us feel? What happens when the feelings we're longing to have fulfilled change, and now the person no longer meets our needs and desires?

There's an old folksy saying that perfectly describes a marriage based on need: It's like two ticks with no dog. Both are trying to receive life from the other, and both ultimately come up dry. We're designed in the image and likeness of the Source of all life, but we are not that Source ourselves. We merely point to and reveal him. One cannot receive from a spouse what can only be received from God.

Ron and Connie were in a desperate situation. Connie thought she had worked through all her insecurities from past abandonment, abuse, and neglect in three broken marriages, but this had clearly not happened. Connie's fear of abandonment led her to self-sabotage, rejecting Ron with rage and childish behavior in an effort to push him away and force him to prove that she was worth rescuing.

Connie truly wanted to be married and didn't want another divorce. But Ron's act of selfless love—marrying her even after her cancer diagnosis—touched that place of pain in Connie's heart and subconsciously drove her to try to disprove that such love was genuine. It sounds illogical, but I have seen it too many times. All too often, couples look to the other to meet their needs for love and affirmation, which produces conflict as they create situations that will test the extent of that love.

The only love Ron had available to give was what he had received from Father God. He knew the deep work the Lord had done in his own life and knew the gospel was powerful enough to transform his wife. That faith, hope, and love manifested through Ron in remarkable perseverance. Ron had his own emotional needs, and they certainly weren't being met by his wife. But Ron had more than enough to give.

The solution to our sense of need is not found in our spouse. Our spouse is a limited resource. It is idolatry to demand from our spouse what can only be provided by God.

Despite his shortcomings and various missed opportunities, Ron stayed consistent in his decision to love his wife toward transformation. And while he would certainly benefit from any change in her life, I believe he truly wanted her to be free for her own sake.

Why do you want to love your spouse? Is it because you're miserable in your marriage right now and hoping that by showing them love, your circumstances will change? If so, it's selfishness and manipulation, not really love. Is it because you're hoping that by showing love, you'll set an example that changes how your spouse treats you? That's just more selfishness and manipulation.

What if your spouse never changes? What if they treat you exactly the same for the rest of your life? Are you so satisfied by God's love that you don't need your spouse to change?

Ron and Connie's story is an extreme example. I'm not recommending that you remain in an unsafe situation. Ron chose perseverance based on an honest conviction of his own safety, not an unwise desire to play hero or martyr. Most of the negative behaviors and attitudes exhibited in marriages do not put anyone in harm's way, and hopefully your situation is nowhere near the severity in this testimony. You don't need to leap to the extreme of divorce over irritating behaviors like bickering, annoying habits, or expressions of contempt. Rather, it's an opportunity to reveal Jesus. Be sure to check with trusted mentors or counselors about what to do in your own situation, and don't let anyone talk you into a level of risk that is beyond your personal convictions and faith.

But I do share Ron and Connie's story to show you what God can do in a situation that is hopefully worse than yours. Ron's choice to love selflessly made all the difference. When you decide that your spouse doesn't ever need to do a single thing for you for the rest of your life, you will finally be free to love them as God first loved us.

Romans 5:6–8 says, "You see, at just the right time, when we were still powerless, Christ died for the ungodly. Very rarely will anyone die for a righteous person, though for a good person someone might possibly dare to die. But God demonstrates his own love for us in this: While we were still sinners, Christ died for us."

God's love doesn't wait for us to change. It *hopes* for future change but doesn't *require* it. Countless people have rejected God's offer of love, but that changes nothing about the way he freely gave his Son for all humanity (1 John 2:2).

As long as we live from a place of need—requiring anything from the other person before we feel fulfilled—all our love will be polluted and broken. Even our most generous actions will be tainted with manipulation, secretly still striving to receive something from the other person. Real love can only happen through us when we are so satisfied by God's love that we no longer need anything from anyone.

Abundance only comes when we tap into the limitless life that flows from God himself. And before you think, *Yes! That's exactly what my spouse needs. They need to be tapped into Jesus so that they have an abundance of love to give to me,* let's remember that we're not supposed to be searching for our fulfillment from them in the first place. We must receive fulfillment directly from God. Release your spouse from the inappropriate demand of making you feel fulfilled.

I'll tell you what happened to Ron and Connie soon.

Life-Giving Love

My relationship with Robin transformed when I decided I no longer needed anything from her. I chose to receive all my fulfillment from the Lord and then love Robin out of the overflow of that heavenly union. I determined to search the Scriptures and truly know my identity in Christ, and the results were stunning.

Previously, I would base my behaviors on how Robin was behaving. I thought that by reacting in the right ways, I could improve my own quality of life. If Robin was on the attack, I stood my ground and fought back. If she was sweet toward me, I wanted to reward her by being sweet in return. These were all behavior management skills I picked up in college when I studied psychology and human development. I thought I could change her by responding in ways that punish negative behaviors and reward positive ones.

It worked in the textbook. It worked with lab rats.

But there were two fundamental problems. First, psychology can help diagnose and influence a problem in the flesh, but it cannot crucify that flesh. It cannot bring resurrection life or produce a new creation. The children I trained to behave rightly in school often behaved differently at home because all I was doing was temporarily managing their behaviors, not changing their hearts. The lab rats that proved the techniques didn't have sinful, broken hearts to overcome. And that brings me to the second problem: My wife is not a lab rat.[5]

---

[5] However, Robin Ann Thomas has initials that have proven to be a comedic goldmine, which my dear wife deeply appreciates.

In her flesh, Robin pushed back against my psychological manipulation. The wounds and fears operating in her unique internal framework were more powerful than any reward or punishment I could employ. I grew exhausted trying to keep her happy.

My belief that my well-being stemmed from her well-being created a new problem in my mind. Such a view implied that her well-being must therefore likewise stem from my well-being, which meant I was responsible to keep her happy. So not only did I feel like I had to respond perfectly to every behavior for *my* sake, I also felt like I needed to maintain *her* happiness. If Robin wasn't happy, I felt like a failure. And whenever I felt like a failure, conflict felt like an out-of-control spiral into oblivion. How could I rescue us out of the tailspin and bring us back to stability if I was already a failure?

This false idea of managing each other's behavior for our own sake is incredibly common. We all do it to one degree or another. Why do we want to change another person's behavior? Sometimes, it might genuinely come from a place of selflessly wanting them to have a better quality of life. But if we're honest, more often it comes from our own desire for a better quality of life.

Death to self includes dying to the demands we place on others. It's death to requiring others to fulfill our needs. Jesus did not come to manipulate us into becoming better servants. Rather, he said, "I have come that they may have life, and have it to the full" (John 10:10). Then, he gives us the liberty to choose what to do with that abundant life. He doesn't force us to respond in gratitude and surrender to his will. But when love is properly felt, it does naturally produce such a response (Luke 7:47).

God's love is life-giving, not life-draining. When I crucified all my need and demand, suddenly Robin found herself in a completely new environment. I found myself doing chores around the house, not to keep her happy but simply because I wanted to bless my wife. She would say, "You don't have to do that," and I would answer, "I know that. That's what makes it love."

If Robin was in a bad mood after I had selflessly loved her, I didn't take it personally. I didn't internalize her behavior as a commentary on my own success or failure as a husband. Instead, she was free to have a bad day, and it changed nothing about who I am. Accordingly, I no longer felt the need to panic over conflict. Suddenly, I found myself feeling stable in our relationship.

I no longer lived my life trying to manage Robin's behaviors. Instead, I dedicated myself to giving her an abundant life. I knew God loved me in this way, and I naturally blessed my wife out of the overflow of what I received from him.

Overflowing, Abundant Love

God is entirely fulfilled within himself—Father, Son, and Holy Spirit, living eternally in perfect union. God doesn't need our love. His love for us is perfect, untainted by need or manipulation. He wants relationship with us but not because he feels incomplete or desperate without us. He simply loves us.

How is it that God is so loving? Love is his identity. Love is not an attribute of his nature; it *is* his nature.

> Dear friends, let us love one another, for love comes from God. Everyone who loves has been born of God and knows God. Whoever does not love does not know God, because God is love. This is how God showed his love among us: He sent his one and only Son into the world that we might live through him. This is love: not that we loved God, but that he loved us and sent his Son as an atoning sacrifice for our sins. Dear friends, since God so loved us, we also ought to love one another. No one has ever seen God; but if we love one another, God lives in us and his love is made complete in us.
>
> This is how we know that we live in him and he in us: He has given us of his Spirit. And we have seen and testify that the Father has sent his Son to be the Savior of the world. If anyone acknowledges that Jesus is the Son of God, God lives in them and they in God. And so we know and rely on the love God has for us.
>
> God is love. Whoever lives in love lives in God, and God in them. This is how love is made complete among us so that we will have confidence on the day of judgment: In this world we are like Jesus. (1 John 4:7–17)

God is love, and Jesus perfectly revealed the Father (Hebrews 1:3). That means Jesus—the embodiment of God—is the embodiment of love (Colossians 2:9). To encounter Jesus is to encounter love in human form.

No one could manipulate him because he didn't need anyone's approval (Mark 12:14). This also meant that all the love he showed was truly selfless, never demanding or expecting that people treat him any particular way. This is the same selfless love he extends to us today.

Many of us look at Jesus's selfless love and think, *Well, of course he can do that. He's Jesus!* But if you no longer live and now Christ lives in you, why would you expect anything other than that same Jesus to act through your life?

God has given us incredible promises that enable us to participate in his divine nature (2 Peter 1:4). We are the body of Christ (1 Corinthians 12:27). Because the Holy Spirit lives in us, our bodies are physical extensions of Jesus in the earth (1 Corinthians 6:15). That means we too have become love in human form.

Notice what the apostle Paul prayed for his readers:

> I pray that out of his glorious riches he may strengthen you with power through his Spirit in your inner being, so that Christ may dwell in your hearts through faith. And I pray that you, being rooted and established in love, may have power, together with all the Lord's holy people, to grasp how wide and long and high and deep is the love of Christ, and to know this love that surpasses knowledge— that you may be filled to the measure of all the fullness of God. (Ephesians 3:16–19)

Do you want to be "filled to the measure of all the fullness of God"? Then you need a supernatural revelation of his love. Our comprehension of God's love is directly related to the measure of love he can express through us. As 1 John 4:19 says, "We love because he first loved us." Our capacity for real, selfless love is simply an overflow of the love we receive from God.

How to Receive God's Love

Certainly, God's love is revealed in the gospel. His love for a sinful world compelled him to send his own Son to rescue us from sin and darkness (John 3:16). All we have to do is believe in him, trusting that what Jesus accomplished on our behalf is enough. We receive God's love by faith.

But God's love is more than a doctrine to be believed. It is real and tangible. God wants us to experience his love, and Jesus told us how: "Whoever has my commands and keeps them is the one who loves me. The one who loves me will be loved by my Father, and I too will love them and show myself to them . . . . Anyone who loves me will obey my teaching. My Father will love them, and we will come to them and make our home with them" (John 14:21, 23).

Obedience is the gateway to experiencing God's love. The trouble is that many of us read this and assume it means we have to perform to be loved by God. But the same John who witnessed and recorded those words from Jesus later wrote, "And this is his command: to believe in the name of his Son, Jesus Christ, and to love one another as he commanded us" (1 John 3:23). It starts with belief and is demonstrated through our love for others. Our love flows from our faith because, apart from Jesus, we can do nothing (John 15:5).

Jesus continued, "As the Father has loved me, so have I loved you. Now remain in my love. If you keep my commands, you will remain in my love, just as I have kept my Father's commands and remain in his love . . . . My command is this: Love each other as I have loved you" (John 15:9–10, 12).

Even though "we love because he first loved us," our decision to love others is directly related to our continued experience of God's love. Some might say this is contradictory. It's not. We start with a recognition of his love by faith. Then we obey. Then we experience his love. His love still comes first; but we remain in that love by loving others.

Notice Jesus said you'll *remain* in his love. You can't remain in something you're not already in. In other words, he loves you first, then you love others, and this obedience keeps you connected to Jesus so you can experience more of his love.

Later, John expounded further, saying, "In fact, this is love for God: to keep his commands. And his commands are not burdensome, for everyone born of God overcomes the world. This is the victory that has overcome the world, even our faith. Who is it that overcomes the world? Only the one who believes that Jesus is the Son of God" (1 John 5:3–5). The obedience required of us only comes from faith. His commands aren't burdensome because we don't obey them in our own strength. We trust God, and he provides the power for us to love others well.

In other words, it's simple. Believe the truth that God loves you, whether or not you feel it. Then, believe that this loving God placed his Spirit in you when you surrendered your life to Jesus. Now, you can trust God to express himself through your life as you yield to his desires. No matter how unlovable your spouse might seem, you have a supernatural capacity for abundant, selfless, life-giving love. So trust God to love your spouse through you, and you will find yourself receiving even more love from God.

I shared this message with my friend Ron time and again as he struggled to keep his flesh crucified and reveal Jesus to his wife. His choice to love his wife kept him anchored in God's love, granting him ongoing stability. The only way to have a never-ending overflow of God's love for your spouse is to keep on pouring out that love.

Victory in Jesus

One o'clock in the morning. I was tired, but I had committed to love these people. I prayed the whole drive to Ron and Connie's house. "Lord, help me not carry my own offense at Connie. Let me only carry your offense so I can speak with your love and perspective."

We sat and talked, listened, cried, and prayed for two hours. No one knew what to do. We just needed God to intervene. I had a stern heart-to-heart with Connie about the impact of her behavior. I reminded them of the gospel. We eventually reached a point of exhaustion and enough peace that everyone could go to bed and sleep. There was relative peace in their home for a couple of weeks before the battle reignited.

Ron and Connie's conflict continued for three years. During this time, Connie's cancer returned twice more, leading to two more surgeries. That third time really scared her. The pressure she put on Ron to comfort her and understand her outbursts intensified. But when we force people to love us, it's hard to experience their actions as real love.

In the latter months of that third year of marriage, the situation reached a point where Ron sometimes left the house and slept elsewhere when Connie's behavior started. This, naturally, poked at the wounds of abandonment that she carried, bringing further escalation of her rage.

Finally, in July 2022, Ron had reached a point when he felt they hit rock bottom, and he no longer felt safe in his own home. The verbal abuse and violent behavior were only increasing. He went for a walk in the woods and cried out to God, asking why this was happening. Why did the marriage have to end? He knew that he needed to stand against Connie's unacceptable behavior and truly felt forced to divorce her, but he hated the whole situation. God strengthened his resolve and spoke to his heart. "Trust me. This is part of my plan."

Ron told Connie that he wanted a divorce, citing her violence, rage, and verbal abuse. The two didn't talk to each other for the next two weeks.

Connie was crushed. In her words, "All I could think about was that I was old, had cancer, and was going to be alone again. I didn't know how I was going to take care of myself without help. I was at the end of *me*. I finally surrendered and decided to totally trust God." She continued, "Immediately, God changed my perspective on everything. I accepted the fact that my behavior got me to where I was and that I was going to let God take it from here. I died to self that week. I gave everything to Jesus—my fear, my cancer, my future, my heart, my tongue, and my life."

Meanwhile, Ron and I talked for some time about what divorce would look like. He said to me, "The worst part about this is I truly do still love her. This would be so much easier if I didn't. And I'm afraid of what it will mean for her. I don't want her to be alone, and I so want her to have a breakthrough with the Lord. I honestly don't know if anyone else will power through to show her Jesus, and I'm worried about her. But I don't know any other way to bring her to her senses."

This was the Father's love that Ron had received, pouring out of him. Despite all his mistakes and occasional sinful reactions over the last three years, Ron's continual humility before the Lord, willingness to apologize for his own sins, and love for God overflowed in love toward his wife.

After two weeks of silence, Ron asked to meet with Connie. She knew it was to discuss divorce arrangements and to tell her how long she had to move out. But instead, Ron told her that he saw the change in her over the last couple of weeks and wanted to try one more time.

Everything changed from then on. God had finally reached Connie's heart. Her entire perspective on life shifted. She no longer took offense to anything Ron ever did or said. She no longer felt the need to be heard but instead had a desire to listen. As Connie puts it, "I saw Ron differently now. I was remorseful for the way I talked to him, the fits of rage I had, and the trauma I caused him." Connie started attending our church again, and their whole relationship turned around.

It has now been two years since Connie's transformation, and I can say as their friend and pastor that it's a night-and-day change. Jesus has truly done a deep work in both of them.

I'll let Connie tell you the rest of the story in her own words:

> Since my transformation, Ron and I have prayed for the Lord to search us both for anything that needs to be brought to the light. Since I am no longer focused on myself, Ron has been able to see some of his own issues to work on. My issues were so big and loud, he didn't have a chance to see his own. So the Lord has been able to show him some issues of pride that were not serving him well.
>
> Our marriage has not only been saved but transformed. Once I put myself aside and started being the wife that I always wanted to be without respect to how Ron was feeling or acting, I quickly got the husband that I had always wanted.
>
> I have learned to let Ron be Ron, no matter what, and just love him the best that I can. I no longer expect anything from him. I have desires and hopes but not expectations. I lean on Jesus for my needs and wants. Jesus—not Ron—is

now my provider. Although Ron provides for me quite well, his love is second to Jesus's love for me.

Ron and Connie's story is nothing short of miraculous. I share it here with you not as an example of how you need to manage your own unique challenges but as an example of God's supernatural power to bring a breakthrough, even when a situation seems impossible. It's not false hope; it's reality. You and your spouse are a different couple with different struggles than Ron and Connie, but God can intervene when you choose to love selflessly, even to the bitter end. You can't do it in your own strength, but the Lord can empower you and lead you along the journey. He is faithful, even if your spouse never changes.

By Grace, through Faith

If you're finding yourself living from a place of need in your marriage, you are likely expecting more from your spouse than you are expecting from God. When put in those terms, it seems absurd.

We know logically that our spouse cannot possibly give us more than God can, but sometimes our hearts have an easier time believing that our most accessible resource is the person we can see, rather than the God we cannot. It's a faith problem.

Every good thing in the Christian life is received "by grace through faith." That means it's a gift from God, unwrapped through active trust. Our salvation comes in this way (Ephesians 2:8). Then we continue throughout the rest of the Christian life in the same way, "strengthened in the faith as you were taught" (Colossians 2:6–7).

Many Christians come to Jesus to receive salvation by grace through faith, but then they start striving in their own effort to maintain their salvation. But Paul corrected the church in Galatia by asking, "After beginning by means of the Spirit, are you now trying to finish by means of the flesh?" (Galatians 3:3). Healthy Christians guard against slipping back into self-effort. We keep the flesh crucified and continue to trust God for new life.

So right now, simply receive God's love by faith. Accept the fact of his love, regardless of whether you've ever had an experience to prove it. Recognize the proof of Jesus's love for you, demonstrated in his life, death, and resurrection. And then, by faith, begin distributing that pure, selfless love to your spouse and others. As you do, you'll begin to experience more and more of God's love, and your life will be transformed into a beautiful expression of Jesus.

Gathering Your Thoughts

Write down your thoughts about these questions before talking to your spouse about this chapter. Talk to the Lord about any shortcomings you see in yourself, and simply trust him to immediately bring forgiveness, freedom, and transformation to your heart.

1. Are there any personal needs or desires you've been trying to fulfill through your spouse that ought to be fulfilled only by God? Prayerfully offer those concerns to the cross and consider them dead.
2. Ask God to tell you what he thinks of you. Write down the thoughts that come to mind. Next, ask him what he likes and values about your spouse. Write down the thoughts that come to mind.
3. What are some specific aspects of your marriage about which you need to trust God?

Conversation Starters

Open up to your spouse about the following topics. Require nothing from them—only give.

1. Share what impacted you most about this chapter.
2. Tell your spouse what you feel God likes and values about them. Next, speak from your own heart about what you like and value about your spouse.
3. Give your spouse permission to be themself and owe you nothing. Verbally commit to loving them selflessly and needing nothing in return.

Ask your spouse the following:

1. What are three things I can do that will make you feel loved?

CHAPTER 3:

The Prophetic Power of Your Marriage

YOUR MARRIAGE PREACHES. THE QUESTION IS, WHAT IS IT saying?

In Ephesians 5, the apostle Paul gave us a beautiful teaching on marriage, and then he basically said, "I'm not really talking about marriage. I'm talking about Christ and the church" (Ephesians 5:31–32). God designed marriage to be a prophetic picture of Jesus and his bride. Earthly marriage is just a fleeting shadow of a far greater eternal reality in heaven, uniting Jesus with his people.

How we understand marriage is directly related to how we understand our relationship with Jesus. It creates a snowball of understanding, for better or worse. How we think about marriage affects how we think about relating to the Lord, and how we think about our relationship with the Lord affects how we think about marriage.

If you think Jesus sits comfortably on his throne and orders us around, leaving us to strive in our own strength to honor him, then your marital relationship is likely to skew in that direction— the husband coming home from work to rest while the wife waits on him and manages the children. If you think Jesus serves us, celebrates us, attends to us, and partners with us, you'll probably develop a relationship that looks more like friendship, partnership, and mutual honor and love.

God designed marriage to be a gospel presentation. When you and your spouse relate rightly to each other, your family and friends see an embodied gospel. Of course, God wants you to have a healthy relationship for your sake and your spouse's sake, but he also wants you to have a healthy relationship for the sake of the world. We must understand the correlation between marriage and the Christian life so your relationship can rightly evangelize.

Most marriages don't have a relationship problem; they have a gospel problem. As we sort out our understanding of the gospel, our own lives are transformed, and our marriages begin to look like Jesus and his bride.

Bone of My Bone and Flesh of My Flesh

Let's start at the end of Paul's teaching on marriage, when he quoted from the creation account in Genesis: "'For this reason a man will leave his father and mother and be united to his wife, and the two will become one flesh.' This is a profound mystery—but I am talking about Christ and the church" (Ephesians 5:31–32).

If Paul sees a "profound mystery" about our relationship with Jesus hidden in God's creation of humanity, then I believe it's a mystery worth uncovering. So let's take a look.

After creating man, God said, "It is not good for the man to be alone. I will make a helper suitable for him" (Genesis 2:18). I used to think that this meant woman was an afterthought—as though God managed to remember to make male and female of all the animals, but then when it came to his favorite creation, it somehow slipped his mind. That doesn't make sense. It's far more believable to me that our all-knowing, all-wise God made man and woman in this way deliberately to teach us something.

So what did God do? He put man into a deep sleep, took part of the man's side (some translations say a rib), and then made woman from that part of the man (Genesis 2:21–22).

When God presented the woman to the man, the man said, "This is now bone of my bones and flesh of my flesh; she shall be called 'woman,' for she was taken out of man" (Genesis 2:23). And then, in the very next verse, we have the words Paul quoted to the Ephesians, saying that it's about Jesus and us.

Do you see the correlation? Jesus died (deep sleep), his side was pierced by a spear (just like the man's side was opened), and the church was born—bone of his bone and flesh of his flesh. We are his body, and we are his bride.

We are the helper suitable for Jesus.

God had a mission for Adam that was impossible to do apart from union with his bride: "Be fruitful and increase in number; fill the earth and subdue it" (Genesis 1:28). The mission was intentionally designed in a way that could only happen cooperatively.

Likewise, God's mission for his Son, Jesus, is intentionally designed to happen through union with us: Make disciples of all nations, reconcile people to God, and destroy the devil's work (Matthew 28:19; 2 Corinthians 5:18–20; and 1 John 3:8).

Mutual Submission

Let's now look at the beginning of Paul's teaching on marriage.

> Submit to one another out of reverence for Christ.
>
> Wives, submit yourselves to your own husbands as you do to the Lord. For the husband is the head of the wife as Christ is the head of the church, his body, of which he is the Savior. Now as the church submits to Christ, so also wives should submit to their husbands in everything.
>
> Husbands, love your wives, just as Christ loved the church and gave himself up for her to make her holy, cleansing her by the washing with water through the word, and to present her to himself as a radiant church, without stain or wrinkle or any other blemish, but holy and blameless. In this same way, husbands ought to love their wives as their own bodies. He who loves his wife loves himself. After all, no one ever hated their own body, but they feed and care for their body, just as Christ does the church—for we are members of his body. (Ephesians 5:21–30)

Many men have skipped over that first sentence and jumped straight to the second. By ignoring the mutual submission that God commands, many have turned the following instruction to wives into a means of oppression. But this first command—to submit to one another—frames all the rest of the teaching, which simply explains some of the ways in which wives are to submit to their husbands and husbands to their wives.

The word *submit* here is translated from a Greek word that, in this context, refers to "a voluntary attitude of giving in, cooperating, assuming responsibility, and carrying a burden."[6] The implication is not forced subjugation but willing service and teamwork. No one is commanded to make another submit but rather to submit themselves.

When Paul taught that the husband is the head of the wife just as Christ is head of the church, we must understand these words in this context of mutual submission. Many of us are comfortable with the idea of our need to submit to Christ in everything, but when we suggest that Jesus has submitted himself to us in some ways, we become a bit uncomfortable. If it weren't in the Bible, it would seem blasphemous.

We all know that Jesus "did not come to be served, but to serve" (Matthew 20:28). But many of us link this concept to his earthly life. Now that he rules and reigns from the highest place of authority at the Father's right hand, some assume that he's done serving. But Jesus is still serving us as the one who "always lives to intercede" for us (Hebrews 7:25).

Others might imagine a future time when Jesus is done serving, instead focusing his attention on ruling and reigning. Nevertheless, Jesus described even the time after his triumphant return, saying, "It will be good for those servants whose master finds them watching when he comes. Truly I tell you, he will dress himself to serve, will have them recline at the table and will come and wait on them" (Luke 12:37). Even in his future ruling and reigning, Jesus still chooses to serve us. There will never be a time when Jesus stops serving his bride.

It feels scandalous. While countless world religions strive to serve their gods, we have a God who serves us—not because we

---

[6] "Lexicon :: Strong's G5292 – *hypotassō*," Larry Pierce, *Outline of Biblical Usage*, Blue Letter Bible, accessed April 16, 2024, https://www.blueletterbible.org/lexicon/g5293/niv/mgnt/0-1/.

deserve it but simply because he is love personified and chooses us as the eternal objects of his affection.

So, yes, a wife is to submit to her husband in everything, not seeking her own interests but rather the interests of her husband. But this is not a command only to women. Paul wrote generically to both men and women, "Do nothing out of selfish ambition or vain conceit. Rather, in humility value others above yourselves, not looking to your own interests but each of you to the interests of the others" (Philippians 2:3–4). Just as a wife is to willingly submit to her husband, a husband is to submit so fully to his wife that it looks like laying down his life in the same way that Jesus sacrificed himself for his church (Ephesians 5:25).

When Jesus surrendered his life for us, we were still his enemies (Romans 5:10). We hadn't repented yet. We didn't deserve his love and, frankly, didn't want it anyway. Humanity was deeply broken in our sin, but Jesus came and took "the very nature of a servant, being made in human likeness. And being found in appearance as a man, he humbled himself by becoming obedient to death—even death on a cross!" (Philippians 2:7–8).

This, husbands, is how we are to serve and submit to our wives. Do not wait for your wife to change before you choose to cherish her. Do not wait for your wife to apologize before you choose to forgive her and serve her. Instead, choose self-sacrifice, just as Jesus did for us.

Headship in the Home

"For the husband is the head of the wife as Christ is the head of the church, his body, of which he is the Savior" (Ephesians 5:23).

Too many have wrongly interpreted these words through the lens of Western society, in which the word *head* might be understood in terms of, say, the head of a corporation. Everyone in that company is expected to fall into line and do what the head says; otherwise, they risk being fired. The head makes all the rules, casts vision, and establishes a culture that must be followed "or else."

Some popular teachings mask this Western idea of authoritative headship behind spiritual-sounding words like *covering*. They might say that when a woman submits to her husband's will, she is protected by his spiritual covering over her life. This sounds far more palatable, but it nonetheless sometimes leads to the same unhealthy fruit of stifled women and domineering men. And, frankly, this concept is not presented in the Bible.

Biblical headship is arguably less about who makes decisions or determines direction and more about who is a source to someone, just as English-speakers sometimes use the word *head* to refer to the source of a river.[7] The first woman was formed out of man, which means man emerged first and then woman followed—much as the head of a baby emerges first before its body.

Evidence is lacking in literature contemporary with Scripture to suggest that the original readers would have necessarily interpreted Paul's metaphor of headship as a reference to male authority.[8] On the contrary, we find philosophers like Aristotle, Plato, and Philo; the followers of Pythagoras; and early church fathers like Irenaeus, Tertullian, and Hippolytus all using language that relates the word *head* to the concept of "source."[9]

Since authoritarian headship is such a popular view and since it stands in opposition to the core concept of mutual submission presented by Paul, let's take a little more time to examine some counterarguments that are more in harmony with the gospel. This may be a little technical for some, but I believe the health of your marriage is directly tied to how you understand this principle.

In 1 Corinthians 11:3, Paul writes, "But I want you to realize that the head of every man is Christ, and the head of the woman is man, and the head of Christ is God." Does this mean that men stand between women and God? Not at all. This passage does not need to be read as a lengthy, interconnected hierarchy. Rather, each phrase can be understood independently of the others.

---

[7] Craig S. Keener, "The Husband as the Head: 1 Corinthians 11:3–6," *Paul, Women, and Wives: Marriage and Women's Ministry in the Letters of Paul,* (Grand Rapids, Michigan: Baker Academic, 1992), Kindle Edition (2012), 1213.

[8] Gordon Fee, "An argument from culture and shame (11:2–6)," *The First Epistle to the Corinthians, The New International Commentary on the New Testament,* gen. eds. Ned B. Stonehouse, F. F. Bruce, and Gordon D. Fee, (Grand Rapids, Michigan: W.B. Eerdmans Pub. Co., 1987), Kindle Edition, 498.

[9] C.C. Kroeger, "Head," *Dictionary of Paul and His Letters: A Compendium of Contemporary Biblical Scholarship,"* eds. Gerald F. Hawthorne and Ralph P. Martin, assoc. ed. Daniel G. Reid (Downers Grove, Illinois: InterVarsity Press, 1993), 375–76.

Remember, the plausible cultural understanding of the metaphor is that *head* means "source." While Jesus is God, we can say that in the incarnation, Jesus was sent by the Father. The Father is therefore the source of the Son. Likewise, through Christ, all things were created (John 1:2). Therefore, Christ was the source— the originator—of Adam. Naturally, Christ made Eve too, but in the larger argument Paul is making in this passage, he emphasizes that woman came out of man.

This verse is not about a special hierarchy of authority where man stands between woman and Christ. Paul finished his argument by fixing the metaphor, eliminating the possible interpretation of an authoritative hierarchy between men and women. He wrote, "Nevertheless, in the Lord woman is not independent of man, nor is man independent of woman. For as woman came from man, so also man is born of woman. But everything comes from God" (1 Corinthians 11:11–12). This, by the way, reinforces the idea that Paul is using the idea of headship in reference to who is the source of whom, not who is in charge.

Paul's words here echo his statement elsewhere that "there is neither male nor female, for you are all one in Christ Jesus" (Galatians 3:28 MEV). This, of course, is not a statement about an erasing of gender differences. Rather, it highlights men's and women's equality in value, destiny, and spiritual authority.

What about Submission?

In Ephesians 5, the Greek word Paul used when he instructed wives to submit to their husbands (*hypotasso*) is the same Greek word Paul used when he described Jesus submitting to the Father (1 Corinthians 15:28).[10] If we are to believe that this word implies an innate hierarchy of differing value or power, then we would have to go against thousands of years of church doctrine on the nature and relationship of the Trinity. The Son is not innately required to submit to the Father. Rather, the Son chose to submit himself (Philippians 2:5–8).

Biblical submission makes more sense as a humble choice by the one submitting, rather than a posture required by one's nature. As stated earlier, this word means "a voluntary attitude of giving in,

---

[10] "Lexicon :: Strong's G5292 – *hypotassō*," Pierce, *Outline of Biblical Usage*.

cooperating, assuming responsibility, and carrying a burden."[11] Biblical submission is voluntary, which means it is chosen by someone who has the liberty to choose otherwise.

And let's remember, Paul's first instruction was to "submit to one another," so it goes both ways (Ephesians 5:21). Even though the Son willingly submits to the Father, the Father has entrusted all things to the Son (Matthew 11:27).

Historical church doctrine states that the Son is co-equal with the Father.[12] The Son glorifies the Father, and the Father glorifies the Son (John 17:1–5). Whatever we believe about headship must be compatible with this truth, because Christ's head is Father God. In fact, the early church fathers Athanasius, Cyril of Alexandria, Basil, Theodore of Mopsuestia, and Eusebius all argued fervently that when Paul said, "The head of Christ is God," this ought not be taken to mean that the Son is in a subordinate position to the Father.[13]

The idea of a man lording over his wife is not part of God's original design for humanity. Rather, it was part of the curse brought because of sin. In Genesis 3:16, God said to the woman, "Your desire will be for your husband, and he will rule over you." This was not God's original desire. His preference was revealed in creation, before this curse was spoken, when woman was a helper.

In Genesis 2:18, God said, "It is not good for the man to be alone. I will make a helper suitable for him." The Hebrew word for *helper* used here (*ēzer*) has nothing to do with subordination or hierarchy.[14] It is usually a term for strength and is often used to describe God as our Helper (Exodus 18:4; Deuteronomy 33:7; Psalm 33:20; 70:5; 115:9–11; 146:5). In other words, the idea that the woman is a helper does *not* mean that the man has all the plans

---

[11] "Lexicon :: Strong's G5292 – *hypotassō*," Pierce, *Outline of Biblical Usage.*

[12] The term *coequal* here is derived from a popular English translation of the Athenasian Creed, which was recited broadly in Christian churches from the early 500s AD. A couple of hundred years before that was the Nicene Creed, which said the Son is "consubstantial with the Father," a term translated from a Greek word that means "of the same substance." In the culture of the Gospels, the religious leaders understood that when Jesus claimed to be God's Son, he was "making himself equal with God" (John 5:18).

[13] Kroeger, "Head," *Dictionary of Paul and His Letters,* 377.

[14] "Lexicon :: Strong's H5828 – *ēzer*," Blue Letter Bible, accessed April 30, 2024, https://www.blueletterbible.org/lexicon/h5828/niv/wlc/0-1/.

and ideas while the woman is responsible only to passively help out. We would never dream of imposing this definition on God, as though we call all the shots and he is left to carry out our wills as a helper to us. Rather, it means we are partners—the wife standing alongside her husband, strengthening and encouraging him (just as God often does for us).

Who Leads Your Home?

Robin and I trust Jesus to lead our home. And based on the unique ways God has gifted us and transformed our lives, Jesus leads our home in some ways through me and in other ways through her. With that as our default, at times, neither Robin nor I know exactly what to do, so we turn to the Lord and seek his guidance. Sometimes he speaks the same solution to both of us, but sometimes he speaks to one or the other, and we willingly defer as we trust that the other has truly heard from the Lord.

I understand that some readers may not have the luxury of a spouse who listens to the Lord. But you can trust God to steer their heart to lead favorably for you (Proverbs 21:1). Even if your spouse is in open rebellion against God, you can trust the Lord to turn it all for your good (Genesis 50:20; Romans 8:28). If you are surrendered to Jesus, then Jesus leads your home, even to the point of your unbelieving spouse being set apart for God's purposes (1 Corinthians 7:14). You can lead the way in righteousness while still willingly serving and self-sacrificing for a sinful spouse as a revelation of Jesus.

The best examples of biblical leadership are less like a king on a throne sending soldiers off to battle and more like a king on the frontlines of battle, making the first kills (so the rest of the army can fight more easily). Biblical leadership is less like a royal financier in a palace, commissioning an expedition into uncharted lands, and more like a pioneer blazing trails so that others can more easily follow in their footsteps. Accordingly, the ways Robin and I share our expressions of Jesus's leadership have nothing to do with barking orders or demanding service. Jesus leads through initiative and self-sacrifice.

Having said all that, I do believe a biblical responsibility belongs uniquely to husbands. As revelations of Jesus in how we relate to our brides, we have a responsibility to take initiative in self-sacrifice. This is how Jesus leads us, and so it is the ideal expression of the gospel in a marriage. Jesus told his disciples to take up our crosses and follow him (Matthew 16:24). In other words, Jesus takes up his cross first, blazing a trail for the rest of us to follow. Remember, husbands are commanded to "love your wives, just as Christ loved the church and gave himself up for her" (Ephesians 5:25).

Even though Jesus is Lord, he doesn't lord over us. He serves us. Jesus—the head of the church—takes responsibility for us and serves us, never expecting us to become subservient drones. Since the husband is a source to his wife, he ought to own the responsibility to take initiative in righteous living.

Biblical headship is less about calling the shots and more about taking initiative to help others thrive, even at great personal risk. And while Jesus can lead through either a husband or a wife, men ought to willingly carry the weight of loving their wives in this way.

In this view, we are not dealing with a matter of value, hierarchy, or even authority. Rather, we are addressing matters of responsibility and initiative within a mutually submitted relationship. It's a matter of men being a source to their wives and leading the way in self-sacrifice.

The head of my home is Jesus, and my wife and I submit to him first. We also submit to each other out of reverence for him. And so that our marriage can be a prophetic picture of Christ and his bride, I willingly take initiative to lead the way in self-sacrifice, not waiting for my wife to self-sacrifice first. I take responsibility for my wife's well-being—not because I'm better than her but because I want to reveal Jesus to her and anyone else who sees our relationship.

Thankfully, my wife is a solid, mature believer who loves, honors, and submits herself to me just as I love, honor, and submit myself to her. But even if she weren't, I would still take the initiative in self-sacrifice. "While we were still sinners, Christ died for us" (Romans 5:8).

The message to men, then, is this: Always try to be the first person to self-sacrifice in the relationship. Wives can certainly lead in this way too. Any woman of faith can reveal Jesus through initiating self-sacrifice. So, wives, don't wait for your husbands to initiate. You too can be the first person to do the right thing. Jesus can lead through either of you. But husbands, you're abdicating your prophetic role if you're passively waiting for your wife to do the right thing before you'll change your words or actions. Take responsibility for the spiritual health of your family, and demonstrate what it looks like to lay down your life as Christ did for his bride.

What Is Your Marriage Preaching?

Your marriage preaches. The way you relate to your spouse reveals a message to each other, your family, your friends, your church, your neighborhood, and the world. Do people see Jesus when they look at your relationship? Or do they see a false gospel of selfishness, manipulation, fear, blame, bickering, mocking, complaining, or other dysfunctions?

Perhaps you're the only spouse following Jesus right now. You may have even found this chapter frustrating, longing for a relationship that looks like Jesus and his bride. Perhaps you wish your husband or wife would read and apply this book, but they're simply not open to something so blatantly Christian. Don't worry. Even if you're the only one following Jesus, Jesus is still the head of your home (1 Corinthians 7:14). And even if you're a wife, wishing your husband would take initiative and blaze spiritual trails for your family, don't worry. Jesus is the true leader of your home, and he can blaze those trails just as easily through you.

There's nothing wrong with a wife taking initiative in self-sacrifice and being the first person to choose love and righteousness. To do so is to be Christlike. So if you're the wife, don't sit around waiting for your husband to step up to his role. Simply do the right thing, even if no one else is. Your relationship might not yet be a perfect prophetic picture of Christ and the church, but your personal life will be a revelation of the gospel that will minister even to your husband. "Wives, in the same way submit yourselves to your own husbands so that, if any of them do not believe the word, they may be won over without words by the behavior of their wives, when they see the purity and reverence of your lives" (1 Peter 3:1–2).

Likewise, if you're a husband of an unbelieving wife, choose to reveal Jesus, and lead the way in self-sacrifice. Immediately after his instructions to the wives of unbelieving husbands, Peter addressed husbands: "Husbands, in the same way be considerate as you live with your wives, and treat them with respect as the weaker partner and as heirs with you of the gracious gift of life, so that nothing will hinder your prayers" (1 Peter 3:7). It's worth noting that "weaker partner" here is not about inferiority, as evidenced by the fact that in the same sentence Peter calls both husbands and wives "heirs." It may refer to physical weakness or perhaps a weakness in social position within that society.[15]

Whatever the case, notice that husbands are to be considerate of their wives and "treat them with respect"; otherwise they forfeit the effectiveness of their prayers. Men, if you want to live a powerful, Spirit-filled life where miracles and answered prayers are normal and regular, then one of the most important actions you can take is to treat your wife with love, honor, dignity, kindness, humility, and respect—dying to self and letting Jesus live through you.

As men and women develop consistency in revealing Jesus to each other, soon our marriages will display the gospel as God intended. As you both submit to Jesus and each other, your marriage will become a prophetic picture of Christ and the church.

---

[15] Craig S. Keener, *The IVP Bible Background Commentary: New Testament, Second Edition,* "Wives and Husbands," (Downers Grove, Illinois: InterVarsity Press, 1993, 2014), 693.

Gathering Your Thoughts

Write down your thoughts about these questions before talking to your spouse about this chapter. Talk to the Lord about any shortcomings you see in yourself, and simply trust him to immediately bring forgiveness, freedom, and transformation to your heart.

1. What are some ways in which your marriage currently resembles Christ and his bride, the church?
2. What are some aspects of your relationship with your spouse that seem to run contrary to how Jesus and his bride relate to each other? Especially consider your own role.
3. Are you rightly relating to and/or partnering with our heavenly Bridegroom? What are some aspects of your own personal expression of faith that fall short of the relationship Jesus wants with you?

Conversation Starters

Open up to your spouse about the following topics. Require nothing from them—only give.

1. Share what impacted you most about this chapter.
2. Tell your spouse some things you see in him or her that effectively reveal the gospel. Especially emphasize the ways he or she relates to you that parallel the heavenly relationship of Christ and the church.
3. Confess to your spouse any areas where you see a need for growth in your own life—whether relationally in your marriage or in your relationship with God.

Ask your spouse the following:

1. What is a dream you have for our marriage that I can help you see fulfilled?

CHAPTER 4:

Seeing What God Sees

WHEN JESUS WALKED THE EARTH, A CERTAIN SECT OF JEWISH adherents distinguished themselves by believing, among other things, that there are no spirits and no one will rise from the dead for a final judgment. They were called the Sadducees.

Jesus, however, boldly taught about the resurrection promised for everyone who knows God. So the Sadducees decided to offer Jesus a logic puzzle, hoping to trick him in his words. They cited a passage from the law of Moses, which commands, "If a man's brother dies and leaves a wife but no children, the man must marry the widow and raise up offspring for his brother." Then they posed an absurd scenario about seven brothers, each dying in succession, until finally, the woman died. Then they asked, "At the resurrection, whose wife will she be, since the seven were married to her?" (Luke 20:27–33).

But Jesus was not bothered by this question. He answered with wisdom, but it was admittedly one of the least romantic answers one could imagine: "The people of this age marry and are given in marriage. But those who are considered worthy of taking part in the age to come and in the resurrection from the dead will neither marry nor be given in marriage" (Luke 20:34–35).

In other words, you didn't marry your spouse forever. You married your spouse "'til death do us part." Surely, this doesn't mean you won't be emotionally close to your spouse in eternity. It simply means that the priorities in eternity are different than the ones here. Marriage is a sacred and special bond, but it's not eternal.

Why, then, is marriage considered so important? Why does God's Word guard marriage so fiercely? Why does God hate divorce and only allow it in a few specific scenarios?

It's because of what marriage represents. It's a mere shadow of a far greater eternal reality. The real, divine marriage is Christ and his church, dwelling in union together forever. Whatever we do in our earthly marriages must not only reflect that divine marriage; it must prioritize it.

This life is a mere microscopic speck on the timeline of eternity. We ought to invest more in the line than the speck. How we manage our relationships and resources here will be directly related to our roles and responsibilities there.

Marriage Is a Spiritual Weapon

God instituted marriage at the very beginning of time. From the first hours of man's existence, God was already preaching about the divine union that would one day come. The gospel message was woven into the fabric of the creation story, pointing ahead to the union of Jesus and his bride, the church.

But marriage is more than a message. Like all prophecies, it is a spiritual weapon (1 Timothy 1:18; Ephesians 6:17).

God's commission to Adam and Eve was not only to multiply but to subdue the earth (Genesis 1:28). To subdue something is to dominate it—to bring it under control. But if God repeatedly called all his creation "good" as he formed the universe, why would the earth outside the garden need to be conquered?

The garden of Eden had a boundary; otherwise, the couple could not have been later cast out of it (Genesis 3:23–24). Everything inside the garden was orderly and beautiful. But what was beyond its borders?

When Satan rebelled in heaven, he was cast down to earth (Ezekiel 28:16–17). Whether this happened before man's first sin or after, God certainly had this idea of humans conquering the devil in mind. Inside the garden, the serpent could only ask questions and lie but could not exert authority. He had to undermine mankind's authority through deception. But throughout the land outside the garden, this spirit could have exercised his will largely unchecked—"a roaring lion looking for someone to devour" (1 Peter 5:8).

God could have obliterated Satan in the blink of an eye. Instead, he cast the devil down to earth and gave mankind the privilege of conquering darkness (Genesis 3:14–15). In the end, the church exercises victory over the devil (Revelation 12:11).

When Adam and Eve were told to subdue the earth, they were not expected to do it alone. They were told to multiply. The Bible's first mention of sex, then, is found in the context of this call to advancing God's rule and reign throughout the world. No wonder our spiritual enemy puts so much attention on tempting mankind with sexual immorality. Sex, in its proper context, is part of the story of mankind's triumph over darkness.

But it's not only about offspring. Paul tells us that anyone who unites with a prostitute—which is not for procreation but for pleasure—becomes one flesh with that person, just as a married couple does (1 Corinthians 6:16). Clearly, a powerful spiritual dynamic is at work even when no babies are being made. God designed sex for the purpose of oneness, honored it by making it an activity that can produce life, and introduced it to mankind as a component of spiritual warfare—advancing his victorious kingdom throughout the earth.

Sexuality aside, all human relationships have spiritual implications. Scripture warns us that anyone who does not love others is partnered with the devil (1 John 3:8–10). It's hard to conquer the devil when you're aligned with him. How you relate to your spouse (or anyone, for that matter) is directly connected to whether you're walking in spiritual victory or defeat.

Naturally, marriage—as the closest and most intimate relationship in your life—is at the top of the list for relationships that affect your spiritual well-being. Your spouse might not have the same spiritual goals, but that's okay because God only holds you accountable for your own actions and reactions. "If it is possible, as far as it depends on you, live at peace with everyone" (Romans 12:18). Remember, your marriage is already perfect. You can walk in victory, enjoying your perfect marriage, even if your spouse is walking in defeat.

Your marriage is a powerful weapon that is advancing one kingdom or another. If you're surrendered to God's heart and choosing selfless love, no matter the consequences, then you will one day stand before the Lord with honor and dignity, knowing that you partnered with him in his victory, standing firm in faith despite the opposition. But if you're focused on yourself—your feelings, your comfort, your reputation, etc.—then you're partnering with the wrong kingdom and need to change course.

You're Not Married for You

Selfishness and pride rob us of a fulfilled life because you weren't created for yourself. You were made in the image and likeness of the God who is love. Your greatest fulfillment is found in being who you were always created to be—a living, breathing expression of love to those around you.

God designed our personal capacity for joy to remain frustratingly incomplete until it is united with Jesus's joy. When his joy enters our hearts, our joy is finally full. And how do we receive his joy? Look at what Jesus said in John 15:10–12. "If you keep my commands, you will remain in my love, just as I have kept my Father's commands and remain in his love. I have told you this so that my joy may be in you and that your joy may be complete. My command is this: Love each other as I have loved you."

His joy enters our hearts when we obey his command to love. As selfishness dies, joy and fulfillment spring forth.

Robin and I found our greatest joy in marriage only after surrendering our right to be made happy by the other. God did not give you a spouse to make you happy. God gave you a spouse so that together, you and your partner can reveal his glory, living as a prophetic picture of Christ and the church.

Jesus's happiness does not depend on his bride's behavior; if it did, he would be mostly miserable. Jesus was happy and fulfilled before we ever came on the scene. Jesus communes with the Father and overflows with love to people who don't deserve it.

Do you want to be happy in your marriage? Stop waiting for your spouse to make you happy. Let the Father lavish his love on you so that you have an abundance to give to your spouse, even when he or she doesn't deserve it. As you pour out selfless love, you will experience the joy of the perfect marriage God has given you. God blessed you with someone to love, serve, honor, and prefer. He graced you with an opportunity to display his heart to someone who is close to you and always present, making them truly challenging to love. And he believes in you and has already given you everything you need to display his glory as you relate to your spouse, no matter how difficult he or she may be.

Seeing What God Sees in Your Spouse

A friend reached out to me for help. She and her husband are both believers, but a series of events had led to serious strain in their marriage. They had been going to counselors and therapists for some time, which was generally helpful. But this day, the counselor gave this woman some advice that didn't sit right with her. She was advised to treat her husband "like an estranged cousin" because of his challenging behavior.

Immediately, my friend thought of Jesus's words: "What God has joined together, let no man separate." She felt the counselor's advice was contrary to what she knew the Bible said about marriage. She reached out to me, wanting to know if she was in error to think and feel this way.

I don't generally speak against the advice of professional counselors, but in this specific case, I agreed with my friend's feelings on the matter. Paul's words in 2 Corinthians 5:16–17 came to mind: "So from now on we regard no one from a worldly point of view. Though we once regarded Christ in this way, we do so no longer. Therefore, if anyone is in Christ, the new creation has come: The old has gone, the new is here!"

If we no longer regard anyone "from a worldly point of view," then that means we regard them from a heavenly point of view. We are seated with Christ in the heavenly realms, after all (Ephesians 2:6). We're commanded to think in a way that prioritizes heavenly reality over earthly reality. Colossians 3:1–3 instructs us, "Since, then, you have been raised with Christ, set your hearts on things above, where Christ is, seated at the right hand of God. Set your minds on things above, not on earthly things. For you died, and your life is now hidden with Christ in God."

Part of dying to our old life is dying to our old perspective. Our old perspective prioritizes self-preservation and achievement. Even self-sacrifice is tainted with selfishness when the old perspective's motivation is to play the martyr and somehow leverage our actions to our own advantage. Real self-sacrifice surrenders the need for any personal advantage that might be gained. Heaven's love values the other above oneself.

When our perspective changes, the ways we treat others naturally change.

One day, my preteen son was squirming, bouncing, and climbing all over my leather office chair. This expensive chair wasn't built for rough behavior. But no matter how many times I tried to explain that to my son, he kept going back into my office and misusing my chair for fun.

After the third or fourth time of correcting him, I said, "Please stop misusing my chair. That was a gift from your Aunt Suzanne."

My son immediately snapped to attention. "Oh! This was a gift? Why didn't you say so?"

I couldn't help but laugh at how my son's behavior changed as soon as he found out the chair was a gift. Telling him that it was expensive didn't motivate him because we've taught our kids that money is nowhere near as important as people. When expensive things break, Robin and I are disappointed but peaceful about it. "It's just stuff," we say. But when the chair was suddenly linked to a person's love, my son saw value in it that transcended its price tag.

When our perspective changes, our behavior changes. My son discovered value in my chair that far exceeded any earthly appraisal. Likewise, heaven sees your spouse differently than the world does.

Heaven sees every Christian as a new creation who carries the Holy Spirit and is therefore free from their past sins and failures. Heaven sees the worst sinner as a person worth dying for and then does something about it. Heaven sees the struggling believer as a new creation who doesn't yet understand their true identity.

Heaven does not see your spouse as an estranged cousin with whom you need to be emotionally distant. Heaven does not prioritize self-preservation. Love "does not dishonor others, it is not self-seeking, it is not easily angered, it keeps no record of wrongs" (1 Corinthians 13:5).

Instead of keeping an account of everything your spouse has done that is contrary to their created purpose, keep an account of the good that God has done in them. Point out and encourage anything in your spouse's lifestyle, character, or behavior that is in line with his or her identity in Christ (or if they're not a believer, affirm anything you see in them that looks like Jesus). The more you point out Jesus in your spouse, the easier it will be for them to believe the gospel and live accordingly.

Freedom to Be

I once worked in an environment where my boss expected me to be incompetent. Admittedly, I didn't know a lot about the business and all that my role entailed. But my boss had been burned by so many incompetent employees that his expectations were low, so he scrutinized and critiqued every action, sometimes making me do a task repeatedly until he was satisfied.

My greatest frustration, though, was not the fact that my boss constantly found fault in my performance. My greatest frustration was that no matter how competent I was in other settings and scenarios, I somehow kept falling short on the job and disappointing my boss. My fear of inevitable disapproval led me to overthink nearly every action. I felt like I was doomed to be a failure on the job, even though this was the only environment where I so consistently performed poorly.

Many people feel this way in their marriages. They're generally competent, emotionally stable people. Perhaps they thrive in the work environment. Maybe their friends love being around them. But somehow, in the presence of their spouse, they keep making mistakes and behaving like someone they don't want to be. Their spouse expects the worst from them, and despite all efforts to the contrary, they keep proving their spouse right.

Contrast this with anyone you've ever been around who truly believed in you. Perhaps it was a parent, teacher, coach, pastor, or some other leader who saw potential and called it out in you. They set you up for success, and you thrived. Even if there was a learning curve, you found the freedom to succeed because someone was cheering you on, encouraging you through the failures, and celebrating your victories.

Which sort of environment is easier to succeed in? Which sort of environment is easier to transform in?

Many people want their spouse to change, so they take the posture of my former boss, critiquing behavior, complaining about the other's incompetence, and generally expressing disappointment. They might even internalize the problem, saying things like, "Why do I always pick such losers?"

In an environment like that, no wonder the person's spouse never changes.

What's it like to live with you? Sometimes we can be so distracted by our experience of our spouse that we never consider our spouse's experience of us. What does your behavior and communication look and feel like to your spouse? You might want to ask them. Do they feel like you're more consistently critical or more consistently encouraging? Do they feel like a failure or a success around you?

One of the greatest gifts you can give your spouse is the freedom to be who they are and to grow from that place. Robin has blessed me so much by expressing admiration (even when I don't deserve it), encouraging me, and refusing to define me by my failures. We've created a home environment where criticism is rare and affirmation is common. We choose to find each other's quirks endearing rather than annoying—laughing about them rather than complaining. And we purposefully expect the best from each other—not in a demanding way but in a liberating way, trusting each other and refusing to punish or demean the other if something doesn't work out.

It didn't happen automatically. It's a habit we deliberately developed. You can develop this habit too.

More than a Conqueror

You may be thinking, *Gosh! If I had a spouse like that, then maybe I could get ahead. That's my problem. My spouse isn't viewing me from heaven's perspective or treating me like Jesus.*

But somehow, Jesus was able to genuinely be himself, even though the leaders in his community, the people of his hometown, and even his own family saw him from a worldly perspective, sometimes actively defying him. The community leaders even plotted his wrongful arrest and execution (and succeeded!), but none of that changed Jesus or held him back from being a revelation of the Father.

Certainly, no one is saying that we are obligated to subject ourselves to consistent emotional abuse. We'll talk about how to establish healthy boundaries in Chapter 8. But right now, I want to give you hope for emotional resilience. When you know God's love for you and have his perspective of you, your spouse, and others, you can withstand a surprising amount of opposition.

While you can accelerate someone's growth by creating the right environment for them to thrive, you are also not bound by the environment created for you by others. Your biggest problem is not the perspective others have of you; it's the perspective you have of yourself.

Whose voice do you rehearse in your head? Your spouse's or the Lord's? Whose statements about your identity do you meditate on? What perspective of yourself do you choose to agree is true?

The gospel offers you an identity shared with Jesus. He is our great High Priest and the King of Kings, and you are part of a nation of priests and kings (Hebrews 4:14; Revelation 19:16; 1 Peter 2:9). He is the Lord our Righteousness, and we are the righteousness of God in Christ (Jeremiah 23:6; 2 Corinthians 5:21). He is the only begotten Son of God, and we are children born of God (John 3:16; 1:12–13). He is the Prince of Peace, and we are peacemakers who sow in peace (Isaiah 9:6; James 3:18). He is seated at the right hand of the Father, and we are seated with Christ in the heavenly realms (Mark 16:19; Ephesians 2:6).

It's not prideful to think of yourself in such terms. It's only prideful to try to leverage your identity to assert yourself over others. Jesus knew exactly who he was and chose to wash feet.

Romans 12:3 warns us, "Do not think of yourself more highly than you ought, but rather think of yourself with sober judgment, in accordance with the faith God has distributed to each of you." This passage does not tell us not to think highly of ourselves, just not *more* highly than we ought. Instead, it tells us exactly how to think of ourselves: with sober judgment, in accordance with faith.

"So then faith comes by hearing, and hearing by the word of God" (Romans 10:17 NKJV). If we're supposed to think of ourselves with faith-based sober judgment, and if faith comes from hearing the word of God, then we are commanded to think of ourselves in line with what God says about us.

James 1:22–24 teaches us, "Do not merely listen to the word, and so deceive yourselves. Do what it says. Anyone who listens to the word but does not do what it says is like someone who looks at his face in a mirror and, after looking at himself, goes away and immediately forgets what he looks like." In other words, God's voice (in the Bible, in prophecies, and in his still, small voice) tells you what you look like. To live any differently is to forget what you look like. The victorious Christian life is mostly found in simply remembering what you look like now that you're a new creation.

Don't internalize what anyone says about your identity if it contradicts the truth God has spoken. It doesn't matter what your spouse says about you. It doesn't matter what your parents said about you. It doesn't matter what the traumas of your past have communicated to you. Choose to prioritize God's voice over all of it, and with time and intentionality, you can become emotionally and spiritually stable.

What, then, shall we say in response to these things? If God is for us, who can be against us? He who did not spare his own Son, but gave him up for us all—how will he not also, along with him, graciously give us all things? Who will bring any charge against those whom God has chosen? It is God who justifies. Who then is the one who condemns? No one. Christ Jesus who died—more than that, who was raised to life—is at the right hand of God and is also interceding for us. Who shall separate us from the love of Christ? Shall trouble or hardship or persecution or famine or nakedness or danger or sword? As it is written:

"For your sake we face death all day long;
we are considered as sheep to be slaughtered."

No, in all these things we are more than conquerors through him who loved us. For I am convinced that neither death nor life, neither angels nor demons, neither the present nor the future, nor any powers, neither height nor depth, nor anything else in all creation, will be able to separate us from the love of God that is in Christ Jesus our Lord. (Romans 8:31–39)

How Does God See Your Marriage?

When God created the first married couple, he had a vision for a victorious church. Certainly, he wanted the couple to enjoy each other and his world, but his vision for the impact of their marriage was so much bigger than their short-lived enjoyment of life.

God has a vision for your marriage too. His dreams for you and your spouse transcend mere companionship or romance. Those experiences are nice and are part of revealing Jesus, but they can also be self-serving. If that's all there is to your marriage, then you will insulate yourselves and squander your potential impact on the world.

In a generic sense, God's vision for every marriage is that we would reveal the gospel by being a prophetic picture of Jesus and his bride. Along these lines, he has called us to make disciples of Jesus while demonstrating his love to each other and the world. Every individual, and therefore every married couple, can accept this as God's plan for their lives.

But in a specific sense, God's vision for my marriage may look different from yours. How we partner with the Lord and engage in his mission can vary widely.

For Robin and me, our first responsibility is to our boys. They're the people with whom we have closest proximity, and therefore, they are the people with whom we have the greatest influence. We know that if we steward our boys well, and if they choose to honor God with their lives, this generational effect will long outlive us, should Jesus delay in returning.

After that, Robin and I open our home twice each week to different small groups of people who want to learn to know Jesus more fully. Robin attends one meeting, and she ministers to children during the second meeting, allowing young families to participate without distractions. Not everyone has to do this, but it's what the Lord has led us to do.

Along those lines, we frequently have different people over for prayer, discipleship, pastoral counseling, or just dinner and fun. Even though I'm very much an introvert, I know the value of choosing relationships over isolation. We know that because our marriage is a prophetic picture of Christ and his church, any time spent with us will result in people being transformed by the gospel we display.

My friends Dave and Paula invited recovering drug addicts to live in their home. My friends Jared and Boggie moved their family to share Jesus and serve people in a foreign country. My friends Dan and Sarita moved to a new city and started a church.

I have many friends who have started church meetings in their homes. Still others serve in a variety of larger churches. Some are bankers, artists, salespeople, mechanics, cashiers, musicians, builders, medical personnel, etc.

My friends Joe and Emily both work regular jobs while also making disciples. Twenty to thirty people come to their home every week to experience Jesus. Meanwhile, Joe oversees home building and renovation crews, and Emily is an ultrasound technician at a crisis pregnancy center. They have three daughters who know the Lord, and they make plenty of time for family and fun.

I know a woman whose husband doesn't know the Lord. She has devoted herself to being the best revelation of Jesus to her husband that she can be. Meanwhile, she prays fervently, is devoted to her church friends, and shares Jesus with neighbors.

You don't have to be professional clergy to make disciples or multiply God's kingdom. You don't even need to have a spouse who is a Christian. You just need to catch God's unique vision for your marriage. Whatever he tells you to do, he will empower you to do.

How God directs you and your spouse may evolve over time. As each of you are conformed more and more into the image and likeness of Christ, the Lord will entrust more and more responsibility to you. Remember, his commands are not burdensome (1 John 5:3–4). Jesus said, "Come to me, all you who are weary and burdened, and I will give you rest. Take my yoke upon you and learn from me, for I am gentle and humble in heart, and you will find rest for your souls. For my yoke is easy and my burden is light."

Gathering Your Thoughts

Write down your thoughts about these questions before talking to your spouse about this chapter. Talk to the Lord about any shortcomings you see in yourself, and simply trust him to immediately bring forgiveness, freedom, and transformation to your heart.

1. What does God think of you? Ask him in prayer and write down the thoughts that come to you. Then take time to discern whether what you wrote aligns with Scripture and the principles shared in this chapter. Is it a heavenly perspective?
2. What does God think of your spouse? Ask him in prayer and write down the thoughts that come to you. Then take time to discern whether what you wrote aligns with Scripture and the principles shared in this chapter. Is it a heavenly perspective?
3. What are some ways I can engage in God's mission, given my current situation in life?

Conversation Starters

Open up to your spouse about the following topics. Require nothing from them—only give.

1. Share what impacted you most about this chapter.
2. Tell your spouse what you feel heaven sees when looking at them.
3. Are there any ways in which you have been overly critical of your spouse and created an environment where success is difficult? If so, confess your sin and apologize.

Ask your spouse the following:

1. What is it like to live with me? Do I tend to make you feel more like a failure or a success?
2. What would be meaningful for you to hear from me that would help you feel like I value and admire you?

CHAPTER 5:

You Become What You Behold

I WANT TO SHARE WITH YOU ONE OF THE WEIRDEST STORIES IN the Bible. It comes from Genesis 30:25–43.

You might know the story of Jacob working for Laban as a sort of dowry to marry his daughter Rachel. Well, to make a long story short, he was able to marry Rachel, and after fourteen total years of work, his obligations were met, and it was time to move on.

But Laban wasn't about to let his best worker leave without protest. Laban realized he was prospering because of Jacob's hard work and God's blessing on his life. He said, "Name your wages, and I will pay them" (Genesis 30:28).

Jacob made Laban an incredible offer. He would to go to Laban's flocks that day and remove all the speckled and spotted sheep and goats as payment, leaving all the spotless ones for Laban. Spotless sheep and goats were more valuable in those days, so this seemed like a great deal to Laban. In the future, any spotless sheep or goat found in Jacob's herd would be considered stolen and returned to Laban.

Laban jumped at the deal—free, ongoing labor from his best worker and spotless flocks for years to come.

But Jacob was a crafty guy. Here's where the story becomes weird.

Jacob, however, took fresh-cut branches from poplar, almond and plane trees and made white stripes on them by peeling the bark and exposing the white inner wood of the branches. Then he placed the peeled branches in all the watering troughs, so that they would be directly in front of the flocks when they came to drink. When the flocks were in heat and came to drink, they mated in front of the branches. And they bore young that were streaked or speckled or spotted. (Genesis 30:37–39)

Not only that, Jacob only displayed the speckled branches when the strong sheep and goats were there to mate but removed them when the weak ones came. As a result, all the weak offspring went to Laban, and all the strong ones went to Jacob. Thus, Jacob prospered even more than Laban.

What Are You Looking At?

What does all this have to do with marriage? Everything. It's a weird story, but it hints at a principle that can be found throughout the Bible, especially the New Testament: We tend to reproduce what we put in front of us. Or, to put it another way, we become what we behold.

The apostle Paul wrote, "But we all, seeing the glory of the Lord with unveiled faces, as in a mirror, are being transformed into the same image from glory to glory by the Spirit of the Lord" (2 Corinthians 3:18 MEV). In other words, as we behold the Lord, we become more like him, going from one degree of expressing him to the next. When we can see who Jesus is, we can see who he is *in* us, which means we can trust him to be that same Jesus *through* us. Our transformation is expressed through faith, trusting the Holy Spirit to do all the work and reveal Jesus through us in ever-increasing measure.

The problem is that we often choose to focus on our spouse's sinful behaviors rather than the Lord and what he is speaking. We wallow in how our spouse makes us feel rather than marveling at what Jesus has done. We meditate on our spouse's history, faults, and failures. But if we become what we behold, then as we behold problems, we become problems.

This doesn't mean we should avoid or ignore problems. It simply means that the problems ought to be peripheral to the glory of God—secondary issues that do not occupy the place of greatest importance in our thoughts. Focus on Jesus as the main attraction, and the problems will be easier to address.

When we focus on our spouse's hurtful words or selfish actions, our flesh naturally wants to punish them—either by doing the same things (so they know how it feels) or by responding in a way that makes us feel mature (but is actually an attempt to manipulate or control our spouse's behavior).

But what if, instead of focusing on our spouse's issues and being affected and shaped by those problems, we focused on Christ and who he is, being affected and shaped by him? Soon we would find ourselves responding as Jesus wants to respond.

Jesus Is a Proactive Forgiver

My friends were at an impasse. This husband and wife were teetering on the edge of divorce because of how hurt the wife had been by the husband's history of lies and emotional avoidance. Despite a long history of growing up in church, they had only recently started hearing the full gospel. God was bringing a spiritual awakening to their family and doing a deep work in their hearts, but the pain of their relational turmoil couldn't be ignored.

The wife came to me for advice. She didn't want to be seen in public with her husband. She didn't want him to come to church with her. The situation at home was bad with seemingly no solution in sight.

If the husband had been sitting in my living room with me, I would have had plenty to say to him, but he wasn't there. I could only work with the wife. And victory wouldn't be found in analyzing the husband's behavior. The wife had been analyzing his behavior for years now, and look where it had brought them.

I turned her attention to Jesus and started to talk about his love and power over sin. And most importantly, I talked about his definition of forgiveness.

"When God forgave you," I said, "he didn't say, 'No big deal. Let's move on.' No. God said, 'What you did was wrong, and a price must be paid. I'll pay it.' And then he sent his Son to die a criminal's death in your place. God's version of forgiveness doesn't shrug off sin. It crucifies it. And it's a proactive forgiveness. It doesn't wait for us to repent. While on the cross, Jesus cried out, 'Father, forgive them, for they do not know what they are doing' (Luke 23:34). He prayed these words before anyone repented or apologized. They were still in the act of crucifying him, and he was already forgiving. And that's how Jesus forgave you."

I continued, "If you want to see what God thinks about how your husband treated you, all you have to do is look at Jesus on the cross, taking that sin into his body and being brutalized as the Father poured out his wrath on that sin. Romans 8:3 says that Jesus 'condemned sin in the flesh.' He killed that sin on the cross, and he paid the full price that your husband deserves. For you to punish your husband or make him somehow pay for what he has done is to say to Jesus, 'The price you paid is inadequate.'"

I added, "Remember that picture of Jesus being tortured, revealing God's wrath against your husband's sin. As I said, that's how God feels about the way your husband treated you. That's also how God feels about your unforgiveness."

I paused a moment to let the gravity of my words sink in. Then I explained that most people struggle to forgive, not because it's difficult but because it's impossible apart from Jesus. Jesus said in John 15:5, "Apart from me you can do nothing." Nevertheless, "With God all things are possible" (Matthew 19:26). Forgiveness is not a strength we find within ourselves. It is a decision to put our unforgiveness on the cross with Jesus, consider it dead, and then let Jesus forgive through us, in the power of the Holy Spirit.

My friend decided to choose forgiveness that day. She put her bitterness and resentment on the cross. I declared to her, "In the name of Jesus, you are forgiven." And then, with help from the Holy Spirit, she voiced her own decision to forgive her husband. We discussed some practical ways to demonstrate her forgiveness to her husband, and then we prayed and she left.

Change started almost instantly. Her husband was shocked and even confused by the genuine shift in her behavior and attitudes toward him. She started speaking words of encouragement and affirmation to him. And soon, his own heart began to soften and change. It's not that the husband's change hinged on his wife's actions—if so, then he would not be responsible for his own sin. But when his wife began to reveal

Jesus to him, even before he deserved it, his heart began to understand the gospel in ways that her bitterness couldn't communicate.

The two of them started coming to church together again, and a process of real restoration began in their marriage. They both sought out and received valuable counsel for their marriage and Christian walks over the coming months, leading to tremendous growth and repentance. Their commitment to do the hard work of dedicated effort in their marriage welcomed God's miraculous work, and it started with beholding Jesus.

Jesus said that God's kingdom is like yeast—a little bit spreads through the whole batch of dough (Matthew 13:33). When my friend beheld Jesus, it not only transformed her more into his image but worked its way into her husband as well. As she selflessly displayed Jesus in her life, her husband beheld Jesus in her and became more like him too.

If you are in a similar situation, I'm not saying that this story will necessarily play out the same way for you. But I share this testimony as a reminder that God is powerful, and we are never exercising false hope when we put our hope in him. We never go wrong when we choose to forgive in God's strength.

But please note: Forgiveness and reconciliation are two different matters. "While we were still sinners, Christ died for us" (Romans 5:8). Forgiveness is a one-sided act. Reconciliation is two-sided. God proactively forgives us, but that's not enough to save us. God's act of forgiveness merely opened the door for reconciliation; it didn't fully accomplish it. Reconciliation requires a humble response to his forgiveness. This is why Paul begged, "We implore you on Christ's behalf: Be reconciled to God." (2 Corinthians 5:20). It's possible to reveal Jesus to your spouse yet not see them respond in the way my friend's husband did. Relational restoration requires two people. Your responsibility is simply to do your part and initiate the process by choosing to forgive like Jesus.

Rethinking Sin

As this story illustrates, one of the most difficult messages to tell a person who has been sinned against is that victims are sinners too. Just as much as God hates the sins that were committed against you, he hates your sinful responses as well. All of it is a distortion of his design.

We were created for something greater. The theologian N.T. Wright defends the idea of God's anger against sin, comparing it to the emotion felt by a violin maker who sees his latest masterpiece being used as a tennis racket. But he continues, pointing out that while many other religions involve humans striving to pacify an angry god, our God proactively moves on our behalf because of his great love for us.[16]

Feelings of condemnation work actively against a healthy marriage. When we know we've messed up, we might cower, hiding in the bushes like Adam and Eve, trying to cover our own shame and avoiding the only One who can fix the problem. We might sense God's anger, wrongly thinking he is fuming in the distance rather than actively reaching out to rescue us. He is a loving Father and wants to set us free.

He knows what you're made for, and he sees sin misusing you. He knows your purpose, and he hates to see you living below the wonderful, fulfilling life he designed.

In Judges 20:16, Israel is said to have had a band of elite warriors who could "sling a stone at a hair and not miss." The Hebrew word for *miss* here is the same word translated elsewhere as *sin*.[17] This is why many have defined sin as "missing the mark."

What, then, is the mark?

To answer that, we can look back before the first sin—before Adam and Eve ate the forbidden fruit in the garden. What do we find there? Male and female, living in union with each other and God, created in his image and likeness.

The mark at which we aim is a life of such union with each other and God that when people see us, they experience him. The mark is being effective image-bearers who reveal the Lord's nature with clarity. Sin, then, is anything short of that original design.

We know from Scripture that Jesus never sinned (Hebrews 4:15; 1 John 3:5). This is why he could say, "Anyone who has seen

---

[16] N.T. Wright, *The Day the Revolution Began: Reconsidering the Meaning of Jesus's Crucifixion*, (New York: HarperCollins Publishers Inc., 2016), Kindle edition, 132.

[17] "Lexicon :: Strong's H2398 – חָטָא / ḥāṭā'," Blue Letter Bible, accessed May 30, 2024, https://www.blueletterbible.org/lexicon/h2398/niv/wlc/0-1/.

me has seen the Father" (John 14:9). A sinless life looks just like God.

Many have argued, "That's Jesus! I could never be sinless. I'm only human, after all." But Hebrews 2:17 tells us that Jesus was made like us, "fully human in every way." If Jesus was fully human in every way but never sinned, that means sin is subhuman. God designed humanity to be sinless, communing with him and bearing his image and likeness on earth. Then he sent his Son to remove our sin (John 1:29; 1 John 3:5).

Too often, we think of sin as a list of activities that we're supposed to avoid. But the problem of sin runs much deeper. If we only deal with surface-level behaviors, we'll never address the identity issue—that we are living below our created purpose.

Made for Glory

Remember, Scripture tells us that as we behold God's glory, we are "transformed into the same image from glory to glory" (2 Corinthians 3:18 MEV). There is a clear link between the glory of God and the image of God. For example, when Moses asked to see God's glory, he was asking to see God's face (Exodus 33:18–20).

Hebrews 1:3 tells us, "The Son is the radiance of God's glory and the exact representation of his being." Jesus lived a glorious life. To see him was to see the Father (John 14:9). He only did what he saw his Father doing (John 5:19). Jesus expressed perfect glory.

But here's where it gets crazy. Jesus prayed in John 17:22–23, "I have given them the glory that you gave me, that they may be one as we are one—I in them and you in me—so that they may be brought to complete unity." Jesus prayed this prayer for all who would believe in him, and it applies to your marriage as well. He wants this perfect unity for your marriage because it's what he wants for the whole church.

If your spouse isn't saved, don't worry. Just behold Jesus, become like Jesus, and reveal Jesus to your spouse. Then they will see Jesus, and hopefully, this will lead to their own transformation.

Jesus gave you the same glory he received. It is possible for you to live according to your original design, revealing the image and likeness of God in everything you say or do. You were made for glory.

The mark—the target—is the glory of God. To sin is to fall short of that glory (Romans 3:23). It is to fall short of revealing God. But remember, apart from Jesus, we can do nothing. God's glory shines from us only as we live in right relationship with him. As Paul revealed in Romans 14:23, "Everything that does not come from faith is sin."

Faith is the opposite of sin. Faith is the means by which we live our new lives in Christ (Galatians 2:20). God has designed the target in such a way that the only way to hit it is by trusting him.

It's like you're shooting a bow and arrow at a target fifty yards away, and no matter how hard you try, your arrows don't even pass twenty yards. Every time you try, you not only miss the mark—you fall terribly short of it. This won't ever change, even with practice or training. The game is rigged. It's impossible for you to hit the target.

But with God, all things are possible. If you will call out to God for help, Jesus will come, wrap his arms around you, take hold of the bow and arrow, and hit the bullseye every time.

Jesus never sins. He has never once missed the mark. How could he do this? Well, for one thing, he is God; but there's a wonderful biblical clue that is more relevant to our lives: "No one has seen the Father except the one who is from God; only he has seen the Father" (John 6:46). Jesus walked this earth as a living, breathing revelation of the Father because he had clearly beheld the Father. And so, we learn in Hebrews 4:15 that Jesus was "tempted in every way, just as we are—yet he did not sin."

In 1 John 3:2, we read, "We know that when Christ appears, we shall be like him, for we shall see him as he is." In other words, a day is coming when we will see Jesus in his fullness and be made like him in his fullness. Until that day, the more fully we can perceive him, the more fully we become like him. This is why, a few verses later, John adds, "No one who lives in him keeps on sinning. No one who continues to sin has either seen him or known him" (1 John 3:6). So according to John, the antidote for our sinful actions is seeing and knowing Jesus.

As you behold his glory, you become more like him. Seeing who he is exposes any areas where you fall short of his glory so that you can surrender them to the cross. Whenever you see an aspect of who he is, it becomes possible to then trust him to reveal that attribute through you. When you live by faith, trusting Jesus to express himself through you, he reveals the Father through you. At each step of your transformation, sin gives way to glory.

A Glorious Marriage

Just as we are individually created to bear God's image and reveal his nature in the earth, so marriage is established to bear the image of Christ and his bride, the church. For the individual, anything less than the image of God is sin. And for the married couple, anything less than revealing Christ and the church is sin.

That's not to say that you should think of your marriage as sinful. Remember, your marriage is a perfect covenant, established by God. And even if your spouse is entirely against God, they are nevertheless set apart for God's purposes because of their sacred union with you (1 Corinthians 7:14). Your marriage is holy because you are surrendered to Jesus. Nevertheless, your relationship may be falling short of the glorious design God has in mind. Acknowledging the intended design gives us a target worth aiming at. And acknowledging our inability to hit the target without Jesus's help positions us to receive his power and be transformed.

Your marriage probably isn't going to start at the point of perfectly revealing Jesus and his bride, but either of you can become a clearer revelation of Jesus to the other, even if the other keeps changing for the worse. Eventually, the hope is that both of you will fully surrender to God and be conformed more and more into the image of the Lord. In time, you'll look like Christ and his glorious church.

The goal of individual transformation is to be made into the image and likeness of Christ. That means a fully formed church—which is comprised of transformed individuals—will one day look just like Jesus together (Ephesians 4:12–13). In that day, bride and Bridegroom will stand together in perfect union, shining with the same brilliance and sitting on the same throne of authority (Revelation 3:21).

Jesus is still King, and we are still nothing without him, but he has welcomed us to rule and reign with him, even to the point of one day judging angels (1 Corinthians 6:3). This is the prophetic picture that marriage is to embody. When I say that marriage reveals Christ and the church, I don't mean as we presently are—

where he is perfect in every way, and we are discovering our identity. Such a view would result in husbands with a superiority complex, thinking only their wives ever need to change. Rather, I mean we are to become a picture of the eternal, victorious King and his pure and spotless bride. If we want to know how to relate to our spouse, look at the eternal destiny of Christ and the church, where we find a holy union of mutual submission, service, honor, love, friendship, intimacy, joy, and partnership.

For my wife and me, this looked like increasingly extended seasons of such glory. Then we'd have a hiccup, work through it by confessing sin and putting our flesh on the cross, and then get back to our glorious marriage.

Remember, your marriage is already perfect, even if your relationship isn't. When you and your spouse experience a relational hiccup, your marriage hasn't changed. It simply means one or both of you is living in your flesh, and you both need to recalibrate your hearts back to living in the Spirit together.

Lowering the Bar

If sin is anything that falls short of the original design—anything that does not come from faith—then a lot more actions and attitudes suddenly become sinful. This definition significantly lowers the threshold of what we call sin, and that's a good thing.

Many of us think of sin as wrong behaviors forbidden in the Bible. Accordingly, we can live a decent life in our own strength—no lying or murdering, for example—and delude ourselves into thinking we don't have a sin problem. Meanwhile, we're just as dead in our transgressions as those who give in to their urges. It's all flesh if it's not faith, and that makes it sin (Romans 14:23).

To put it another way, I was raised by wonderful, godly parents. They raised me to be compassionate, thoughtful, and kind. But one day, I realized that no matter how thoughtful, compassionate, or kind I was, it still paled in comparison to Jesus's thoughtfulness, compassion, and kindness. So if I wanted Jesus to express those virtues through me, then I needed to die even to my virtues and trust the Holy Spirit for something better. As the prophet Isaiah declared, "All our righteous acts are like filthy rags" (Isaiah 64:6).

In Galatians 2:20, Paul did not say, "My bad behaviors have been crucified with Christ." No. He said, "*I* have been crucified with Christ and *I* no longer live, but Christ lives in me" (emphasis added). That means every bit of self-effort must go to the cross. Everything that does not come from faith—even the virtues— must die.

There's a simple, practical reason for this. As long as I misunderstand sin as only a list of bad behaviors, then, when I have a love deficit, a joy deficit, a gentleness deficit, or whatever else, I am left to assume that the solution is to try harder—striving in my own effort rather than trusting Jesus. But when I call those deficits sin, the solution becomes clear: confess my shortcoming, consider it dead, and trust the Holy Spirit to reveal Jesus through me. Suddenly, Jesus starts hitting the mark on my behalf, and I find myself revealing the Lord.

The work is already done. Jesus meant it when he declared, "It is finished!" (John 19:30). In other words, I have to see that even though I'm in the process of being made holy, I'm also already perfect in Christ. Hebrews 10:14 says, "For by one sacrifice he has made perfect forever those who are being made holy." If I don't see that I'm already complete in him, then when I find sin in my life, I feel inadequate and am left to try harder next time. But if I know that I'm already a new creation—that the old is gone and the new has come—then I simply need to crucify whatever falls short of his glory and live according to the truth of who God made me to be when I was born again (2 Corinthians 5:17).

> So I tell you this, and insist on it in the Lord, that you must no longer live as the Gentiles do, in the futility of their thinking. They are darkened in their understanding and separated from the life of God because of the ignorance that is in them due to the hardening of their hearts . . . .
>
> That, however, is not the way of life you learned when you heard about Christ and were taught in him in accordance with the truth that is in Jesus. You were taught, with regard to your former way of life, to put off your old self, which is being corrupted by its deceitful desires; to be made new in the attitude of your minds; and to put on the

new self, created to be like God in true righteousness and holiness. (Ephesians 4:17–24)

Scripture invites us to put off the old independent self and put on the new self, which partners with Christ and thrives in the power of the Spirit.

The same goes for your marriage. Put off the lies that your marriage is broken, struggling, or hopeless. Contemplate the prophetic picture of Christ and his church, and crucify whatever exists in your own heart that is contrary. Lay hold of your new self and therefore your perfect marriage, and simply live accordingly. Give your spouse opportunities to succeed (which means giving them opportunities to fail). Particularly if he or she is a Christian, expect them to live as a new creation. And like a loving brother or sister in Christ, if they do something sinful, confront them humbly and privately (Matthew 18:15). And do it as one who sees them from a heavenly perspective.

Choosing Glory

Sometimes a wife chooses to follow her husband not because her husband is necessarily right or holds more power or value but because she desires to show what it looks like for the church to humbly submit to our Lord and trust him. This also means that sometimes a husband chooses to follow his wife not because she is necessarily right or holds more power or value but because he desires to show what it looks like for Jesus to humbly lay down his own interests for the sake of his bride. In a kingdom marriage, a husband and wife can race each other to be the first to reveal Jesus through submission, humility, and honoring the other above oneself.

Peter emphasized the Old Testament figure Sarah's obedience to her husband, Abraham (1 Peter 3:6). But we also have examples of the patriarch Abraham obeying Sarah (Genesis 16:2; 21:9–12).[18] The Bible doesn't give us a clear-cut instruction that one gender is always supposed to rule while the other is always supposed to submit. On the contrary, the Bible only gives a clear-cut instruction that *I* am to serve and love my spouse, demanding

---

[18] Keener, *The IVP Bible Background Commentary*, 693.

nothing in return. In other words, the responsibility to submit does not belong to only one gender; it belongs to *you*, regardless of your gender (Ephesians 5:21).

Don't wait for your spouse to do what you feel their gender role requires of them. Whether you are a husband or a wife, your first thought in any situation shouldn't be, *What is the perfect role for a husband or a wife in this situation?* Instead, it ought to be, *What does Jesus want to do in this situation?* Why? Because the endgame of the bride's transformation is to "become mature, attaining to the whole measure of the fullness of Christ" (Ephesians 4:13). The eternal bride looks identical to her Bridegroom.

Be a revelation of Jesus to your spouse. And as you continue beholding Jesus and becoming more like him, you and your spouse can eventually find yourselves surprised by a harmonious relationship. With intentional love and death to self, your marriage will look more and more like Jesus and his beautiful bride.

Gathering Your Thoughts

Write down your thoughts about these questions before talking to your spouse about this chapter. Talk to the Lord about any shortcomings you see in yourself, and simply trust him to immediately bring forgiveness, freedom, and transformation to your heart.

1. What narrative most often occupies your mind when it comes to your marriage? Are you focused more on the problems that exist in your relationship? Or are you focused more on who Jesus is and what he is doing?
2. What is the biggest challenge you're facing in your relationship right now? Picture Jesus in the same scenario. What does Jesus want to do?
3. In what areas of your life do you fall short of God's glory because you've been acting independently rather than in faith?
4. Are there any situations in which you've been too focused on the problem, making Jesus secondary, rather than focusing on Jesus and making the problem secondary?

Conversation Starters

Open up to your spouse about the following topics. Require nothing from them—only give.

1. Share what impacted you most about this chapter.
2. Have you recognized any sin in you that falls short of God's glory? Confess it to your spouse and apologize for misrepresenting Jesus to them.
3. Have you been fighting for your rights in any area of your relationship rather than choosing to submit as a revelation of Jesus? Express your heart about the matter to your spouse, being honest about your fears, concerns, or insecurities. But then explain what you see about Jesus's nature and how you want to reveal him in this scenario.

Ask your spouse the following:

1. What is one area of my life that you think might be a blind spot for me—an area where I might think I'm okay but that doesn't actually look like Jesus?

2. In reference to the above, what does Jesus look like that stands in contrast to my behavior? Let's take time to consider him together, describing his nature and giving our hearts time to soak in the truth of who he is.

CHAPTER 6:

Reverence for Christ

Y EARS AGO, I MINISTERED BRIEFLY IN THAILAND. ONE OF THE locals warned me of an obscure law there. He said that because it is shameful in their culture to show the bottom of your foot to someone, if you drop a Thai coin on the ground, do not give in to your instinct to step on it to keep it from rolling away. The king's face is on that coin, and to step on the king's image is to step on the king. Such an offense is punishable by up to fifteen years imprisonment.[19]

Human beings, both male and female, are created in the image and likeness of Christ (Genesis 1:26–27). Even when we aren't walking in close fellowship with God to rightly display that image and likeness, we still all bear the same intrinsic value. Like a Thai coin, your spouse bears the image of our King, even if he or she isn't particularly effective at it. And as Thai law illustrates, how we treat each other is how we treat the one whose image we bear.

In Matthew 25:31–46, Jesus spoke of the final judgment, comparing it to a shepherd separating sheep from goats.

> "Then the King will say to those on his right, 'Come, you who are blessed by my Father; take your inheritance, the kingdom prepared for you since the creation of the

---

[19] Jill Robbins, "Eight bizarre laws around the world are why it pays to do your travel homework," My Journal Courier, July 2, 2023. https://www.myjournalcourier.com/news/article/bizarre-travel-laws-18169821.php.

world. For I was hungry and you gave me something to eat, I was thirsty and you gave me something to drink, I was a stranger and you invited me in, I needed clothes and you clothed me, I was sick and you looked after me, I was in prison and you came to visit me.'

"Then the righteous will answer him, 'Lord, when did we see you hungry and feed you, or thirsty and give you something to drink? When did we see you a stranger and invite you in, or needing clothes and clothe you? When did we see you sick or in prison and go to visit you?'

"The King will reply, 'Truly I tell you, whatever you did for one of the least of these brothers and sisters of mine, you did for me.'"(Matthew 25:34–40)

The king went on to reprimand another group, saying that whatever they did *not* do for others, they did not do for him. To neglect others is to neglect Christ.

If this is true of "the least of these," surely it is true of your own household. You may recall that Paul's instruction about mutual submission was directly tied to one's honor of Jesus. "Submit to one another out of reverence for Christ" (Ephesians 5:21). How you treat your spouse is how you treat Jesus.

Pleasing Jesus

As a United States citizen, I have lived my entire life as a resident of a culture where our political leaders work for us (or, at least, are supposed to). Here, we don't think much about serving or pleasing our leaders unless, perhaps, you're a lobbyist trying to garner favor for your cause.

But in the culture of the Bible, having the king's favor could be the difference between life or death. The Scriptures recount the history of various people who found favor with kings—such as Joseph, Esther, and Daniel—which led to the saving of countless lives.

In the kingdom of God, our King "opposes the proud but shows favor to the humble" (James 4:6). Our God actively stands against those who think they deserve or merit any sort of aid from him. Instead, he shows his power on behalf of those who know and admit their desperate need. We serve a God who says, "My

78

grace is sufficient for you, for my power is made perfect in weakness" (2 Corinthians 12:9). We have our King's favor, not because of our performance but because we are his children and depend on him.

I generally favor my kids too, but their words and actions can either please or displease me. I'm always proud of them and always celebrate them, but they can take specific actions that bring joy or disappointment to my heart. The same is true of God. This is why Scripture instructs us to "find out what pleases the Lord" (Ephesians 5:10).

In the church's divine marriage with Jesus, our role is to "seek first his kingdom and his righteousness," and his role is to then look after our needs (Matthew 6:33). We delight ourselves in the Lord, and he gives us the desires of our hearts (Psalm 37:4). In the kingdom, we seek the fulfillment of his needs and desires, and he seeks the fulfillment of our needs and desires.

Whenever we seek after the fulfillment of our own desires, we rob God of the opportunity to bless us, and we rob ourselves of the joy of receiving something God can do far better than we can. It's a trust problem. We think we're better at taking care of ourselves than he is. And it's a pride problem. Humility looks like dependence.

This is the relationship that marriage represents. The healthiest marriages look like seeking the fulfillment of each other's needs and desires while trusting the other to reciprocate. It's intentional interdependence.

Intentional Interdependence

I'm a pastor, a traveling minister, an author, and a publisher. Meanwhile, my wife is a computer programmer and teaches horseback riding lessons to kids at her parents' family business. Our career choices could not be further apart. But Robin helps me pastor, encourages and makes time for my writing, does all the bookkeeping for my traveling ministry and publishing company, and fills online orders from my website. Meanwhile, I often help her problem-solve programming puzzles, take care of our boys while she works outside the home, and build and modify websites for her family's businesses. Sometimes I find myself at the family farm feeding baby animals, driving a hayride, or saddling horses.

Neither one of us ever says, "That's your job, not mine." Instead, we are constantly looking for ways to help each other fulfill our dreams, even when it seems like a distraction or diversion from our own agendas. In fact, we regularly trust the other to show up for us. Intentional interdependence has become our priority.

Jesus doesn't technically need us, but he willingly submits the fulfillment of his greatest desires to the context of union with us.

You can tell what a person's greatest desire is by what they sacrifice for the most. The guy who spends every paycheck on car parts and spends every waking moment tinkering with his old car in the garage is communicating something about his greatest desire. Maybe it's the car. Or maybe it's what the car represents—for example, time spent with his son or daughter. But his greatest sacrifice of time and money is a key indicator of his greatest desire.

What did God sacrifice for the most? Souls—and not only ours but the souls of all humanity (1 John 2:2). His will is that none should perish and that all would come to repentance (2 Peter 3:9). Jesus "wants all people to be saved and to come to a knowledge of the truth" (1 Timothy 2:4).

Think about it. Jesus could snap his fingers, appear to every lost person on the planet, preach the gospel to them, and do it better than you or me.

But he doesn't.

Why?

He wants to do it *with* us.

That's what we see happen at the end of Mark's Gospel. "After the Lord Jesus had spoken to them, he was taken up into heaven and he sat at the right hand of God. Then the disciples went out and preached everywhere, *and the Lord worked with them* and confirmed his word by the signs that accompanied it" (Mark 16:19–20, emphasis added).

Again, Jesus has submitted the fulfillment of his greatest desire to the context of union with us. One could even say that the one thing Jesus wants more than the salvation of the entire world is union with his bride.

Before Jesus went to the cross, his last sermon to his disciples was all about union (see John 14–16). In the middle of this most important message, Jesus said, "I am the vine; you are the branches. If you remain in me and I in you, you will bear much fruit; apart from me you can do nothing" (John 15:5). You may recall from chapter 1 that we don't call grapes the fruit of the branch; we call them the fruit of the vine. The branch without the vine produces nothing. In other words, the fruit that we bear is not our own—it's Jesus's.

Shortly after, Jesus added, "You did not choose me, but I chose you and appointed you so that you might go and bear fruit—fruit that will last—and so that whatever you ask in my name the Father will give you" (John 15:16). Jesus chose you to bear his fruit. Again, he could evangelize the world more efficiently without you, but he chose partnership with you. He could heal every sickness on the planet with a wink of his eye, but he wants you to lay hands on the sick. He could make money pour out of the mouths of a million fish to provide for all the poor, but he wants to love and serve them through you. Jesus has surrendered his own fruitfulness to the context of union with you.

Jesus is intentionally interdependent with us. Just as much as we *actually* need him, he *chooses* to need us. We rely on him, and he relies on us.

The more Christlike person in your marriage is, therefore, not the more independent. Rather, it is the one who more deliberately entrusts their heart and life to the other, no matter how untrustworthy or incompetent the other might be. The goal is being more concerned with giving your spouse the opportunity to fulfill your desires than you are with having those desires fulfilled.

The Fight for Independence

Modern culture celebrates independence. Many of us grew up in a world where we were taught to be proud of doing everything ourselves. Certainly, at some milestones in a child's life, independence is important, like feeding oneself, dressing oneself, toileting, or tying one's own shoes. A certain amount of self-sufficiency is necessary if we're going to be competent to serve others. But even in settings where we teach teamwork, like a children's sports team, many kids still tend to track statistics, each longing to be the most valuable player.

Our culture generally wars against interdependence. It's often seen as weak to need another person. Your own mind and theology might be warring against this idea right now. Perhaps you're thinking back to chapter 2 and how love does not come from a place of need. Doesn't that contradict this point?

On the contrary, it strengthens it. Jesus doesn't need us, but he does choose us. He is completely at rest in the Father's love, not demanding anything from us before he will lavish his love on us. But he also chooses to make himself vulnerable to us. This is perhaps the most loving thing he can do. He welcomes us into his world and prioritizes partnership with us over the fulfillment of his greatest desires. He chooses to need us in the least needy way possible. He doesn't technically need us, but he does wholeheartedly depend on us.

One of the ways Jesus loves us selflessly is by risking himself to us. He entrusts his reputation to us. He entrusts his desires to us. He entrusts his own fruitfulness to us. And he invites us to reciprocate.

Naturally, you may be questioning the wisdom of such deliberate trust. Certainly, in some areas, our spouse is simply not trustworthy. But I would suggest that they are no more untrustworthy than Jesus's bride, and yet he trusts us.

Having said that, communicate with each other and follow the Holy Spirit. Your spouse may not want you to entrust some responsibilities to them, in which case they are trusting you. Some expectations are unrealistic. For example, we could never rightly bear the responsibility to judge the world, so Jesus keeps that responsibility (Romans 2:1–4; 12:19). But he does trust us to judge ourselves and each other so that we can be spared from such divine judgment (1 Corinthians 5:12–13; 11:28–31).

We learn from the parable of the stewards that God trusts us realistically, according to our ability (Matthew 25:14–15). But in that parable, we learn that the king still entrusted one bag of gold, worth about nineteen to thirty-two years of a day laborer's wages, to a servant who completely failed at their task (Matthew 25:24–30).[20] No matter how untrustworthy we are, Jesus still risks himself to us and entrusts world-changing matters to us. Real trust requires

---

[20] Keener, *The IVP Bible Background Commentary*, 112. Keener states that this one bag of gold would have been worth six to ten thousand denarii, each of which was roughly a day laborer's standard wage at the time. Subtracting Sabbaths, that leaves 313 days each year with which to calculate the value. The NIV footnote on Matthew 25:1 conservatively suggests a value of twenty years of wages.

risk. And that means we will need to trust our spouse in an area where they are capable and have the opportunity to succeed, even if you know they will probably drop the ball and fail. Real love risks and is also there afterward to help pick up the pieces.

I can completely trust my wife because I ultimately trust the Lord more than her. That may not sound particularly romantic, but it is honest. If my wife fails at some task I entrusted to her, God is there to help with the aftermath. I must find primary security in my relationship with my Heavenly Father. That's the only way I can be truly secure with my spouse. Humans fail. But God commands us to bear each other's burdens and rely on each other, so failure to trust others is failure to trust God (Galatians 6:2). Our trust in God makes our trust in people safe.

Surrender any need you might have for total independence. Put your distrust on the cross. Trust the Lord enough to trust your spouse. Surrender control for the sake of union.

Voluntary Service

When Paul commanded husbands and wives to "submit to one another out of reverence for Christ," nothing about his command instructs either spouse to subjugate the other. In fact, while similar household codes in Greek and Roman culture included instructions to husbands to keep their wives humble and subservient, Paul contradicted the prevailing culture by inviting both spouses to willingly submit.[21] The moment submission is demanded or required by one party, that party has ceased to submit. Mutual submission only works without demand.

There is never a moment when it is appropriate to tell your spouse that they're supposed to submit to you. Your own voluntary submission precludes this. If your spouse is not serving you and submitting to you, the solution is not found in behavior modification but in heart transformation. What they need most is to be transformed by the power of the Holy Spirit, not conformed into a role of your choosing. In order for their service to be real, it must be voluntary.

---

[21] Craig S. Keener, "Why Paul Told Wives to Submit—The Social Situation of Ephesians 5:18–33," *Paul, Women, and Wives: Marriage and Women's Ministry in the Letters of Paul,* (Grand Rapids, Michigan: Baker Academic, 1992), Kindle Edition (2012), 2362–545.

Good News for Your Marriage ~ Art Thomas

The moment you demand submission or service is the moment you rob yourself of the opportunity to know if your spouse's heart is in it. You'll always be left wondering, *Are they doing this because they want to or because I put up such a fuss about it?* I'm not saying you shouldn't communicate your needs or desires. But what sort of pressure are you exerting to acquire such service from your spouse?

Instead of pressuring your spouse to self-sacrifice, model self-sacrifice. Since we become what we behold, show your spouse what a consistent lifestyle of self-sacrifice looks like so they can behold Jesus and perhaps become more like him.

But don't play the martyr. If you keep pointing at all the sacrifices you've made, hoping that drawing attention to them will earn you credit that coerces your spouse into action, then you're still relying on self-effort and not self-sacrifice. Real self-sacrifice requires nothing in return. Voluntarily serve your spouse, and just as quickly, surrender the need for recognition or reciprocation. Love selflessly. The way you treat your spouse, who bears Christ's image, is the way you treat Christ. When your spouse is loved with no strings attached, your spouse is free to truly love you in return.

Gathering Your Thoughts

Write down your thoughts about these questions before talking to your spouse about this chapter. Talk to the Lord about any shortcomings you see in yourself, and simply trust him to immediately bring forgiveness, freedom, and transformation to your heart.

1. First, describe how you want to treat Jesus. What does he deserve from your life? Second, what are some ways you can treat Jesus this way, recognizing that how you treat your spouse is how you treat him?
2. Are there any situations in which you have been deliberately choosing independence, keeping your spouse at a distance? In what ways, practically speaking, could you willingly begin to depend on your spouse?
3. What is one way in which you could serve your spouse that is not presently expected or required of you?

Conversation Starters

Open up to your spouse about the following topics. Require nothing from them—only give.

1. Share what impacted you most about this chapter.
2. Have you identified any situations in which you have not been treating your spouse the way Jesus deserves to be treated? If so, apologize to your spouse and express your desire to love and serve Jesus by loving and serving them.
3. Let your spouse know that you choose to trust them. Be specific about the situations you've identified where you will exercise such trust.

Ask your spouse the following:

1. Are there any areas in which you don't feel like I trust you completely?
2. What could I do to better communicate my trust in that situation (or those situations)?

CHAPTER 7:

The Best Security System

I'VE ALWAYS BEEN FASCINATED BY RUBE GOLDBERG machines—those overcomplicated chain-reaction devices that usually accomplish an unnecessary task. A clock hand knocks over the first in a line of dominos, which pushes a marble off a ledge into a funnel, dropping it onto a paddle wheel that spins an axel, unwinding a string that lowers a cookie into a glass of milk. It's silly, whimsical, and generally pointless.

When I was ten, I created a security system for my room. I rigged a piece of string that ran from my door, across my room to a light fixture, and then down to a low shelf in my closet. Between the light fixture and my closet was a small stuffed clown with a baseball tied to his belly, carefully hanging from the string near the light fixture, barely held in place by a small knot in the string.

When the door was opened, the string became slack enough for the clown to slip past the knot and ride down the steeply angled string like a zipline. The baseball attached to his belly would knock a cup of marbles off a pedestal in the middle of my room, sending the cup and marbles raining down on a large plastic lid that once covered a cake. If anyone opened my door, they were met with a loud and startling crash. And my ten-year-old sense of humor loved every second of it.

It wasn't much of a security system, but it didn't matter. I didn't need to protect my room from any actual criminals because our house was already secure from outside threats. If our home was not a secure place to live, I might have needed to take matters into my own hands to feel safe. Instead, I was free to goof off and have fun.

But some children grow up in homes that aren't safe. Perhaps there are outside threats, but more often, there are inside threats. Parents, siblings, or caregivers might be rage-filled, hypercritical, or emotionally unstable. Many children grow up not knowing how the primary people in their lives will behave at any given moment. Others learn to predict exactly what will set those people off, feeling the pressure to control the environment to keep the peace. The instability and volatility of the home force them to learn coping skills and defense mechanisms that give them some sense of security.

I grew up in a home with wonderful parents who loved me and the Lord. But no parents are perfect, and even in a relatively stable environment, I, too, learned to defend myself against their weak moments. Whenever I saw that tension was rising between my parents, I learned what sort of well-timed jokes would make them laugh and bring the world back to stability. I learned what sort of behaviors would garner attention or compassion when I needed to escape their critiques. Beyond the home, I learned how to carry myself in a way that calmed those around me rather than irritating them, helping maintain the peace. I also learned how to weaponize my social skills and fight back effectively when cornered. I could use sarcasm and wit like a sharpened blade.

As I grew older, control felt like safety. If I wasn't in control, that meant other people were too unpredictable, so I often retreated into hiding. This manifested later in life as a mild social anxiety and an avoidance of large groups when I wasn't in charge. My favorite relational situations were those where I could exert enough social influence to control other people's emotional states and keep everyone happy and stable.

This became the pattern in my most important relationships. When Robin and I started dating, I did everything possible to control her perceptions of me and keep her happy. I strived to perform, acting like a stellar boyfriend—bringing flowers, opening doors, taking her to her favorite date locations, buying her gifts, writing her love songs and mushy greeting cards, and speaking kind words to her.

I wasn't faking my love and affection—that much was real. But my perfectionism was just a performance. The real me was deeply flawed, and often those flaws came to the surface in the worst possible ways. I often spoke or acted, whether intentionally or accidentally, in ways that conflicted with the sparkly image I was projecting.

If I felt I couldn't salvage my right standing with Robin, I deflected and blamed to make her look comparatively worse than me, always attempting to control the narrative and excuse my behavior. If that didn't seem to work, I apologized to escape the discomfort of the conversation, hoping I could hide behind a simple "I'm sorry" and move on. Then, if all else failed, I exploded in anger, emotionally pushing Robin away and hoping to shut her down.

It was a faulty security system. Unlike my childhood clown-zipline, it wasn't a joke. I didn't feel safe, and the only way I knew to make myself feel safe was to employ my defense mechanisms, no matter who they hurt.

False Security

We all look for a sense of security in our relationships. And whenever we don't find it, we take matters into our own hands, relating to people in unhealthy ways to ease our sense of insecurity.

This looks different for different people. My insecurity manifested as control and avoidance. Both were emotionally easier than letting down my guard and simply trusting others. I sought security in isolation. Avoidance, hiding, and escape were more comfortable than confrontation or the hard work of helping someone else process their feelings. Even my attempts at control were actually avoidance, not being able to trust other people's emotions unless guided by my careful manipulation.

Robin, on the other hand, took an opposite approach. She searched for security in relationships. Her defense mechanisms often appeared avoidant—shutting down emotionally and hiding—but it was always with the hope that someone (usually me) would chase her. Rejection was devastating to my wife, and my avoidant behaviors were crushing to her. When I was stable and performing, she felt secure as I lavished her with affection. But when I shifted into defense mode, my antics yanked the rug out from under her, leaving her hurt and vulnerable, and therefore leading to her own insecure behaviors.

Like me, many people look for security in solitude. Others, more like Robin, look for security in intimacy. Both are insecure positions that lead to desperate behaviors, self-focus, and complications in our most important relationships, especially marriage.

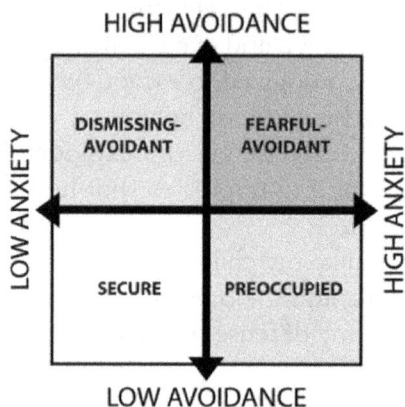

HIGH AVOIDANCE

	DISMISSING-AVOIDANT	FEARFUL-AVOIDANT	
LOW ANXIETY			HIGH ANXIETY
	SECURE	PREOCCUPIED	

LOW AVOIDANCE

Psychologists call these ways of relating *attachment styles*.[22] Attachment styles are measured along two axes: anxiety and avoidance. In the previous example, I measured high in avoidance and low in anxiety, which meant I preferred to be alone. Robin, on the other hand, was high in anxiety and low in avoidance, which meant she craved closeness. One could argue that we both displayed anxious and avoidant traits from time to time, but our primary expressions seemed to skew in those two directions.

Unlike Robin and me, a person who is low in anxiety and low in avoidance is considered *secure*. But like Robin and me, those who are high in anxiety or avoidance (or, in rare cases, both) are considered *insecure*. No one likes identifying themselves as insecure, but recognizing our weak spots is often the first step to transformation.

Generally speaking, we all tend to exhibit some combination of secure, avoidant, and anxious behaviors. Most people fit a primary category, but some can express blends of different types.[23] It's not too important to exactly categorize yourself or your spouse and perhaps more important to be able to identify insecure

---

[22] Attachment styles were originally studied in infants. The concept was popularized by John Bowlby (1969) and Mary Ainsworth (along with her colleagues, Bell and Stayton, 1971). In more recent decades, the research has been expanded to include adults.

[23] Stan Tatkin, Psy.D., *Wired for Love: How Understanding Your Partner's Brain and Attachment Style Can Help You Defuse Conflict and Build a Secure Relationship*, (Oakland, California: New Harbinger Publications, Inc., 2011), Kindle Edition, 47.

behaviors, no matter what form they take. Attachment styles are not your identity.

When you can see that your spouse is not lashing out at you because you're bad or they're evil, it's easier to have compassion, realizing they're struggling with insecurities—either seeking intimacy in an unhealthy way or trying to avoid it out of fear. Which is it? The easiest way to tell is by what direction you were moving when your spouse lashed out. Were you trying to engage? Then they're probably avoiding. Were you trying to disengage? Then they're probably anxious. Recognizing your spouse's insecurities is a secure behavior and worth practicing, even if you're struggling with your own insecurities.

In the study of attachment styles, someone who is highly avoidant, like I was, tends to exercise extreme independence, often withdrawing or hiding. And when that isn't possible, they might lash out at the other to push them away and maintain distance. In my case, I normalized my avoidance by calling myself an introvert. The truth is, I do generally thrive on my own—learning, thinking deeply, expressing creativity, relaxing, and so on. But I often used healthy introversion as a cover-up for my unhealthy avoidance of intimacy.

On the other hand, a person who is highly anxious, like Robin, is often preoccupied with relationships and what the other person is thinking, always longing to draw closer. Her natural extroversion—preferring to learn, think, create, and relax in groups—often masked her desperation to find security in intimate relationships.

In most situations, Robin and I both presented as mature, emotionally stable people. But when it came to our most important relationship—our marriage—our insecurities rose to the surface. Insecurities rarely manifest in relationships where long-term intimacy isn't expected. People can be completely different at work and at home. They can look mild-mannered at church and like rabid animals in the car with their spouse.

Attachments matter most in the home environment, where stability should be experienced. But insecure patterns learned in childhood often follow us. The ways we learned to relate in the primary, inescapable family relationships of our youth become the same methods we employ in later close, committed relationships.

Sometimes, attachment styles go undetected until the relationship becomes officially long-term and established. Some couples never experience each other's attachment styles until they're married. All too often, people have told me about their spouse completely changing on the honeymoon or even on the drive home from the wedding. Prior to that moment, the commitment wasn't real enough to activate the person's insecurities.

When I fell for Robin, I was all-in from the beginning. In our very first conversation about dating, I told her that if she ever wanted to break up with me, she would have to initiate, because I was in this for the long haul. I meant it too. But between my avoidance and Robin's anxiety, neither of us was finding any real security in our relationship, so we both built faulty security systems in our separate worlds, resorting to unhealthy behaviors in a search for some sense of security.

The Anxious-Avoidant Snowball

Robin and I overcame what some consider the most volatile relational setup—a highly anxious person marries a highly avoidant person. You and your spouse may be in a much different scenario. In fact, a little more than half the population exhibits a secure attachment style, being naturally attuned to their partner's needs and providing relational security as an emotionally trustworthy person.[24] But we all have our learned defense mechanisms, and understanding a worst-case scenario can give you insight into your own unique situation. If there's hope for Robin and me, there's certainly hope for you.

When a highly anxious person like Robin experiences a threat to the relationship, they will cope by trying to get closer to their spouse (even if by retreating, in hopes they will be chased). Meanwhile, when a highly avoidant person like me experiences a threat to the relationship, they will cope by emotionally distancing themselves from their spouse.

---

[24] Amir Levine, MD, and Rachel S. F. Heller, MA, *Attached: The New Science of Adult Attachment and How It Can Help You Find—and Keep—Love* (Los Angeles: TarcherParigee, 2010, 2011), Kindle Edition, 8.

The anxious person grasps after a sense of security by trying to *activate* intimacy while the avoidant person seeks a sense of security by trying to *deactivate* intimacy.

In our case, I would say or do something foolish, and Robin would run, hoping I'd chase her. But I wouldn't chase her because engaging in conflict was too emotionally exhausting and I was more comfortable alone. She was craving intimacy, and I was avoiding it.

This left Robin feeling abandoned, which made her angry. And naturally, her expressed anger only made me want to retreat further. I'd offer an empty apology to escape the discomfort of the moment, but she could see through my behavior, recognizing I still wasn't giving her the intimacy she wanted and needed.

As you can see, the anxious-avoidant relationship frequently becomes an unhealthy feedback loop that grows like a snowball. The anxious spouse presses closer, and the avoidant spouse retreats. The anxious spouse experiences more intense feelings of abandonment or neglect, causing them to push even harder for intimacy. The avoidant spouse then naturally feels like they can't escape. The insecure behaviors spiral in a vicious cycle until someone either explodes or crashes in a depressive breakdown.

Thankfully, Robin and I were able to escape the cycle. It took time, but we got there. If you and your spouse are stuck in the anxious-avoidant snowball, there's hope for you too.

Freedom from Insecurity

Psychologists say that attachment styles generally remain stable over time, but they can still be intentionally changed.[25] Secure behaviors can be learned. And of course, God can transform hearts.

As I've asserted before, psychology is great for helping us understand the flesh, but it can't crucify it. Only the gospel produces a new creation. Both the human nervous system and the Scriptures share the same Author, so there ought not be any conflict when studying both. Instead, when properly understood with help from the Holy Spirit, psychology and the Scriptures can work hand in hand. Psychology can give us insight into the reasons

---

[25] *Ibid*, 163.

we behave the ways we do, often indicating people we need to forgive or traumas that need to be confronted with truth to counteract the lies we learned in those experiences. And then we apply the gospel, forgiving offenders and accepting truth, which bring lasting change.

In Robin's and my case, we certainly employed some learned skills as we discovered how to love each other, but the greatest transformation came from our shared discovery of the gospel. Rather than looking to me as her primary sense of security, Robin learned to receive that security directly from the Lord, trusting his love and faithfulness first. Meanwhile, rather than trying to find my own sense of security in isolation and retreat, I too learned to anchor myself in the Lord, crucify my fear of intimacy, and open my heart to my wife and others.

I'm all for professional therapy and counseling, but Robin and I didn't have the self-awareness or wisdom to avail ourselves of professional help. We learned our secure behaviors not from a therapist or counselor but by observing secure couples and encountering Jesus, discovering who he is, considering ourselves dead, and letting the Lord live through us.

As the gospel gradually took root, I learned not to avoid intimacy by avoiding conflict but instead to dive headfirst into it. I learned not to avoid intimacy by isolating myself but to deliberately let my wife (and others) into the most vulnerable places in my heart. These changes happened simply because I saw who Jesus is. Jesus engages in conflict to draw people closer; he doesn't run and hide. Jesus opens his heart to us. Imagine that—God makes himself emotionally vulnerable to his creation. It sounds wrong, and yet this is why it is possible to grieve the Holy Spirit (Ephesians 4:30). As I beheld Jesus, I became more like him.

Meanwhile, Robin saw that while Jesus invited people into intimacy, he didn't chase after anyone for his own sense of security or demand that they chase him. Multitudes rejected him, and he was still emotionally stable (John 6:66–67). Jesus knew his Father's love and rested in that truth, not requiring anything from anyone. As Robin beheld Jesus, she became more like him.

Attachment styles are not our identity. They're not even part of it. Attachment styles are products of our past, but we are to be products of Jesus's resurrection life. All our insecurities need to be surrendered to the cross so that we can trust wholeheartedly in the Father's love for us. True security only comes from him.

We all need to forgive our parents for whatever environments they created where we learned our insecurities. And we all need to confess the sinful judgments that we formed in response to those environments.

I formed sinful judgments that my role is to keep the peace for everyone around me, that I'm only truly safe when I'm in control, and that intimacy is too complicated and exhausting to pursue. And Robin formed sinful judgments that she is an afterthought, that important people don't see her value, and that she's not stable unless the most important people in her life are stable.

But as Robin and I surrendered our sinful judgments to the cross and as we forgave our parents and siblings for their inevitable shortcomings in our early home environments, the lies that informed our insecure attachment styles began to crumble. Resurrection life from the Holy Spirit started to spring up in our hearts and minds. We began to search for our security in the Lord first and to trust the Lord's work in each other, experiencing his love and presence in our relationship as well.

Fight, Flight, or Freeze

Robin's and my insecure behaviors had been manifestations of our own fight-or-flight reflexes. All humans experience this physiological reaction when faced with a threat. Unfortunately, our brains can't effectively discern the difference between a real and a perceived threat. Your brain responds essentially the same way to a rattlesnake as it does to a look of contempt from your spouse. We either fight or run away (or freeze while we try to figure out whether to fight or run away).

The amygdalae in the brain are two almond-size glands that release a cocktail of hormones when we experience threats of various kinds. Meanwhile, the prefrontal cortex—the rational part of our brain—is overwhelmed by the wave of feelings, leaving us functioning almost entirely on emotion and adrenaline.[26] As long as

---

[26] John J. Ratey, MD, *A User's Guide to the Brain: Perception, Attention, and the Four Theaters of the Brain*, (New York: Pantheon Books, 2001), 311–14.

Robin and I didn't feel secure in our relationship, we behaved irrationally in fear, even to the point of hurting the most important person in each of our worlds—something neither of us ever wanted to do.

Survival mode is generally self-centered. That's the nature of trying to survive—self-preservation. Lifeguards understand that a drowning victim will pull them underwater in a desperate attempt at survival. With rare exception, no one in survival mode is thinking about others. Fight-or-flight is all about ending the threat, even if the threat is someone we love.

One of the hallmarks of a secure attachment style is the ability to be attuned to the emotional needs of others and put them first, purely for their sake. But this isn't possible when insecurity clouds our perception and makes our primary motivation the fulfillment of our own unmet needs.

Robin and I fought and fled, pursuing and retreating, all in a desperate attempt to experience the peace we both longed for but couldn't find. Later, when we found that peace in Jesus, we could finally think more clearly and see the other's needs.

You see, the problem was never technically the other person. The problem was the lies we learned through traumas and challenges—strongholds of the mind, which are mental structures formed out of thoughts and ideas that conflict with knowing Jesus (2 Corinthians 10:4–5). Robin had come to believe the lie that unless people saw, understood, accepted, and desired her, she wasn't safe. Meanwhile, I had come to believe the lie that intimacy and vulnerability are unsafe, assuming I can only be secure through either control or isolation. But the gospel confronted these lies, shattered the strongholds, and showed us a better way.

Freedom from fight-or-flight starts with identifying the traumas that trigger our survival reflexes. In my case, a lot of my intimacy issues had more to do with my brother than my parents. He was fifteen years older than me and left home when I was three. I was devastated. He was my best friend, and then he suddenly left. I learned that opening my heart to someone who is supposed to be a permanent relationship can be a painful experience. Robin's situation, meanwhile, was probably mostly rooted in her family dynamics as the youngest of three, feeling left out of her older siblings' friendship, and longing for closeness.

96

We'll talk more in the next chapter about how Robin and I disarmed the triggers. For now, I simply want to build hope for your situation. As Robin and I brought our past traumas to the Lord and dealt with them, we both started to mature—spiritually, emotionally, psychologically, and relationally.

Soon, something amazing happened. Robin and I started to find security in our relationship. As each of us gradually became more stable, we exhibited less selfishness and became more attuned to each other's needs. I became a clearer revelation of Jesus to my wife, which gave her a sense of being seen, known, and loved. And Robin became a clearer revelation of Jesus to me, helping me open up and trust that I was safe in her presence. Our intimacy grew until we became each other's best friends and our anxious-avoidant relationship felt like a distant memory. We've now been in a healthy, secure relationship for well over a decade.

The Two Shall Become One

As Robin and I revealed Jesus to each other, we learned to trust each other. And with those feelings of trust came active dependence upon each other. As noted in the previous chapter, intentional interdependence is healthy, as long as we find our primary sense of stability from the Lord.

Scientifically speaking, spouses become physiological pairs. The ways we interact affect stress hormones. Those spouses in healthy, committed, secure relationships tend to help regulate each other's blood pressure and enjoy better health overall. In stressful situations, our spouse's expressions of empathy can soothe our nervous systems and help regulate heart rate, muscle tension, and more.[27] (Remember that the next time you're in an argument.)

Much literature exists warning of the dangers of codependency, but the term itself is unscientific and often misapplied. The word first emerged in addiction studies back in the 1970s, but definitions (both then and now) vary so widely that it has become unhelpful. Of primary concern is that the way the term

---

[27] Jason N Linder, PsyD, "The Psycho-Physiology of Relationships: What You Don't Know," Psychology Today, July 12, 2020.
https://www.psychologytoday.com/us/blog/relationship-and-trauma-insights/202007/the-psycho-physiology-relationships-what-you-dont-know.

is often applied, people can start to think that it's unhealthy to depend on each other in a relationship, leading to unnecessary and destructive isolation and independence.[28]

A need to be needed is generally unhealthy, especially when that sense of need lends itself to enabling someone struggling with addiction. Likewise, self-sacrifice and service are unhealthy when they come not from a place of overflowing, abundant love but instead from a place of desperation or a fearful attempt at maintaining a fragile relationship. This can lead us to cater to unhealthy behaviors and to fear appropriate and necessary confrontation. But neither of these examples of unhealthy codependency mean interdependence is bad altogether. On the contrary, it's necessary.

Biblically speaking, human beings are more interconnected than Western culture might lead us to believe. In the Old Testament, whole nations sometimes suffered loss because of only one person's sin (i.e., Joshua 7). In the New Testament, we're each accountable only for our own sin (Jeremiah 31:29–34). But we're still interconnected enough for the apostle Paul to be inwardly burdened by the sin of others (2 Corinthians 11:29). The apostle commands us to "carry each other's burdens" and thereby "fulfill the law of Christ" (Galatians 6:2). Friendship and unity in the church are so vital that if we take communion while engaging in divisiveness and cliquishness, we eat and drink judgment on ourselves (1 Corinthians 11:17–24).

Thankfully, Scripture requires relational health only so far as it depends on us (Romans 12:18). If other people refuse peace even after our best heartfelt attempts at reconciliation, our consciences need not be troubled. But this seems to only apply outside the church. When it comes to our fellow Christians, we must pursue relational wholeness until either a person repents or they are removed from the church altogether (Matthew 18:15–20).

Interpersonal relationships are so important that God doesn't even want to receive our worship unless we've addressed whatever conflicts or offenses might be lingering among us (Matthew 5:23–

---

[28] Parisa Soltani, "Unpopular opinion: The myth of codependency," Live Healthy, November 30, 2022, https://livehealthymag.com/unpopular-opinion-the-myth-of-codependency/.

24). In other words, your and my spiritual health is directly related to our relational health.

This is why God does not answer the prayers of husbands who disrespect their wives (1 Peter 3:7). If relationships matter so much to the Lord that he refuses our worship until we attempt to reconcile, then certainly peace must be prioritized in one's marriage. We actually do need to learn to rely on each other.

While I have my own interests, my own career path, my own hobbies, and even some friends who my wife doesn't spend as much time with as me, I still live for my wife's happiness. I choose to serve her. If any of those interests, hobbies, jobs, or friends were burdensome to my wife, I would choose her ahead of my own preferences. I've become the sort of person my wife can rely on, and our relationship is one in which she can find security.

To be clear, my wife's emotional well-being is not my burden, but it is my responsibility. I can't spend all day focusing on keeping Robin happy, as though that were my role; but I must not neglect her either. I aim to be attentive to her emotional condition and compassionate toward her in all my decisions and actions. This doesn't mean I compromise on righteousness to cater to her insecurities—sometimes difficult decisions must be made for the Lord. But I'm still aware of her feelings. I always consider how my actions will affect her. And I aim to always act in love.

I had to develop this skill over many years of raw communication and intentional practice. Robin was patient with me, seeing that I really wanted to serve her well, even though I failed consistently for years on end. She celebrated every baby step of growth and thanked me when I got it right. In time, I learned to love her and became a secure person for her to rely on. And she did the same for me.

If you or your spouse struggle with an insecure attachment style of anxiety or avoidance, there is hope for you and your relationship with each other. You're not codependent, but you are interdependent, and you can both learn to be trustworthy people who can be relied upon. You can develop security in your relationship. You simply need to bring your sinful judgments, anger, and unforgiveness to the cross so you can disarm the triggers and walk in resurrection life.

Gathering Your Thoughts

Write down your thoughts about these questions before talking to your spouse about this chapter. Talk to the Lord about any shortcomings you see in yourself, and simply trust him to immediately bring forgiveness, freedom, and transformation to your heart.

1. Consider the times when you have felt insecure in close relationships. If you can't identify such a situation, then you probably have a secure attachment style. But if you can remember such times, do you tend to try to engage in intimacy to obtain security? Or do you tend to withdraw from intimacy to obtain security?
2. If you identified an insecure attachment style (avoidant, anxious, or both), ask the Lord when or how you learned to seek security in that way. See if anything comes to mind. If you need to forgive anyone in your past, do so.
3. Ask the Lord to help you identify your spouse's attachment style. If it is insecure, what can you do to help them feel secure during times of stress or conflict? Pray for the ability to love your spouse and offer security rather than taking their insecure behaviors personally.
4. In moments of high stress, do you find yourself more often fighting, fleeing, or freezing? Ask the Lord for the grace to reveal Jesus in those moments of stress, and trust the Holy Spirit to help you in the future.

Conversation Starters

Open up to your spouse about the following topics. Require nothing from them—only give.

1. Share what impacted you most about this chapter.
2. Tell your spouse what you have identified about your own attachment style. If needed, apologize for any ways that you have hurt your spouse as your attachment style drew

insecurity to the surface and exerted more influence over your behavior and emotions than the Holy Spirit.

Ask your spouse the following:

1. Do you generally feel like you need more space from me or less?
2. Is there anything I can do for you that will make you feel more secure in our relationship?

CHAPTER 8

Disarming Triggers

IF I WERE TO POKE YOU IN THE ARM WITH MY FINGER, YOU might wonder what I was doing, but it probably wouldn't elicit much of an emotional reaction. However, if you had a large, gaping wound on that arm, you might recoil your whole body and lash out at me in anger.

Whenever we overreact to a small stimulus, it's evidence of a wound. Many people call these wounds *triggers*. No one likes to be triggered. Some go to the work of informing their friends and families about their triggers, hoping those who love them will avoid setting them off. We may even, with time, identify the people who trigger us most often and avoid them. But what do we do if the person who triggers us most is our spouse?

Identifying the Problem

A trigger sets off a release of energy. In a mouse trap, the trigger releases the power of a tightly coiled spring. With a gun, the trigger ignites an explosive that propels a bullet. The problem isn't the trigger. Triggers are harmless. If the trap isn't set or the gun isn't loaded, you can poke and pull the triggers all you want, and there will be no reaction. The problem isn't the trigger; it's the stored-up energy. If we can address what sets the trap or loads the gun, we can render the triggers powerless.

My wife and I like to watch action movies. A classic trope is to make an element of the story the nuclear launch codes that only the president of the United States can access. If someone can launch the USA's nuclear weapons, they can effectively ignite the next World War—or even end the world completely.

In these films, various layers of security prevent an unauthorized launch. Perhaps a key or a computer chip has to be inserted into a machine, and maybe two or three codes from different people need to be entered into a computer. The computer might be in a subbasement of the White House or in a locked briefcase, handcuffed to the wrist of a Secret Service agent. Whatever the case, the consequences of unleashing such weapons are so world-altering that the triggers are protected at all costs.

The less we trust ourselves and the more we fear the unleashing of our inner rage, the more intensely we might guard our triggers. For example, when I was about seven or eight years old, I was sexually abused by some older boys in my neighborhood. For a little over a decade, I avoided boys my age or slightly older. All my closest friends were either at least a year younger than me or at least three years older. I felt too much anxiety around those who even subconsciously reminded me of the past pain I experienced. And whenever one of the wrong-aged people became too close, I either started avoiding them or ended up pushing them away with angry outbursts.

Rage is generally a fear response. It's a learned behavior that is usually connected with self-protection. Some grew up in homes where rage was modeled as a means of exerting control over others. Then, later in life, when a situation feels out of control, even an otherwise well-mannered person might revert to the only tool they know for gaining control: an explosion of rage.

Hopefully, we know that our rage is inappropriate and can hurt others the same way we were hurt in our past, so we try to keep it all inside. We try to avoid situations where our rage might escape, or we might desperately try to employ anger management techniques to restrain our inner beast.

Soon, all of life becomes an adrenaline-pumping action movie where an inner hero wrestles a world of villains next to a big red button. We fight to maintain control and prevent a war. The more we can keep the villains out of the room, the safer we feel. So we remove the so-called toxic people from our lives and guard the doors vigilantly—only letting in those we consider safe.

When you married your spouse, you saw them as safe. You let them in. But now that they're in the room, you find them either dangerously close to your buttons or even bumping into them or intentionally pushing them from time to time. You find yourself exploding at them in ways that you might never treat any other person. Eventually, you might conclude that he or she is the problem and finally file for divorce.

But your spouse isn't the problem. Neither are the triggers. The problem is the stored-up energy.

Again, triggers are harmless. The problem is all the armed warheads that you're fighting so hard to protect. The problem is the rage that you unleash, the panic you spiral into, the bitter darkness that engulfs you, the self-harm you resort to, the mean remarks, the running and hiding from your problems, the regrettable words and actions, or whatever else your warheads look like. The problem is the stored-up energy that is released whenever your spouse stumbles into your launch button.

Why do we spend so much time and effort guarding harmless triggers? Such work is exhausting and lonely. Would it not be better to disarm the warheads and render the triggers powerless?

Triggers Unleash Sin

I try to help my kids identify their triggers so they can understand why they feel the ways they do. This also helps them understand the unhealthy people in their lives, building compassion and revealing what fuels those people's behaviors. I also tell my boys, "Triggers aren't excuses."

Triggers explain our actions, but they don't absolve us of responsibility. No one will stand before God at the judgment and find pardon for sin by pointing at the triggers that prompted their behaviors. "But, Lord, you don't understand. I was abused as a kid!" That's tragic, yes. It should have never happened. But we cannot allow our past to have more authority over our lifestyle than the Holy Spirit.

In Galatians 6:14, Paul wrote, "May I never boast except in the cross of our Lord Jesus Christ, through which the world has been crucified to me, and I to the world." The world includes the painful events that happen to us because our world is fallen. Therefore, I am crucified to the traumas of my past. That means they have no more access to me. The person who was traumatized died, and now Jesus lives in me. Also, the traumas of my past are crucified to me. That means I can no longer draw from them as a reason for living or behaving a certain way. I can no longer point to them as an excuse for my sin. They are inaccessible to me.

When my wife or anyone else bumps into a trigger and I respond by expressing my insecurities, it simply shows me still another area of my heart that has not yet surrendered. I don't become angry that someone pushed my button. I become grateful that I found out about another warhead that has yet to be disarmed. The trigger only exposed the sinful attitude that was already there.

Praise God for our triggers! They help us identify areas of our hearts that are still operating in independence from the Lord.

I still have all the memories of the wrongs done to me. Those stories remain. But those stories have also been redeemed by recognizing what Jesus did to conquer the heartaches, injustices, and lies. If I didn't have those memories, I wouldn't ever be able to share the testimonies of what God has done. I am free from those past events because of the cross of Christ. They are part of my biography, but they are not the last chapter.

Boundaries vs. Walls

We don't win against triggers by pushing people away and avoiding difficult relationships. We win against triggers by bringing our sin to the cross and trusting the Holy Spirit to express Jesus through us. We bring difficult people close to us, and the Lord uses them to expose our sinful condition. Emotional walls are not the answer.

Boundaries and walls are different. Boundaries facilitate healthy relationships; walls prevent them. Boundaries help people connect with us appropriately; walls avoid connection entirely. Boundaries welcome people into our lives and prioritize healthy relationships. Walls push people away.

Boundaries define the borders of the playground and say, "Come play in here with me." If someone crosses a boundary, they are leaving the playground. So when you say, "I'm sorry you don't want a healthy relationship with me," you're not rejecting the person. You're merely pointing out the fact that they left the playground of healthy relationship.

Throughout the process of being conformed into the image and likeness of Christ, the borders of your playground will expand. You'll be able to explore new territory because regions that were once scary have become safe as triggers were disarmed. It's fine to say to someone, "I haven't yet become like Jesus in that area, so please don't push me into it before I'm ready." Simply recognize that this region is worth enjoying, so expanding your boundary into an area that is objectively healthy and appropriate ought to be a goal for you.

Healthy boundaries help us engage in healthy relationships, and they help us identify when others don't want healthy relationship with us. That doesn't mean we need to avoid such unloving people entirely. Jesus still interacted from time to time with the Pharisees, but he didn't welcome their antagonism into his inner circle. Jesus welcomed anyone to follow him, but he also defined the terms of the relationship. Those who were trying to kill him were not joining him in the playground. They were excluding themselves. He didn't give them much attention, except to occasionally rebuke them.

Jesus's example of trust is challenging. For example, he entrusted his moneybag to a thief (John 12:6). He taught us,

> Love your enemies, do good to those who hate you, bless those who curse you, pray for those who abuse you. To one who strikes you on the cheek, offer the other also, and from one who takes away your cloak do not withhold your tunic either. Give to everyone who begs from you, and from one who takes away your goods do not demand them back. And as you wish that others would do to you, do so to them . . . . But love your enemies, and do good, and lend, expecting nothing in return, and your reward will be great, and you will be sons of the Most High, for he is kind to the ungrateful and the evil. Be merciful, even as your Father is merciful. (Luke 6:27–31, 35–36)

This is not an invitation to normalize physical or emotional abuse, but it is a command that Jesus empowers us to obey as he leads us. Jesus did what he saw the Father doing, which meant that he sometimes withdrew, sometimes engaged, and sometimes submitted to mistreatment. He surrendered to the cross, but he didn't let the crowd in his hometown throw him off a cliff (Luke 4:29–30).

We can obey Jesus's command to love our enemies while at the same time enforcing healthy boundaries. Remember, boundaries define and invite healthy relationship. They also help us see when others don't want such a relationship so that we can give them space accordingly. Be led by the Spirit about when to stand your ground and when to suffer well, but don't let well-meaning Christians who don't understand the severity of your trial convince you not to hold the other person accountable for their actions.

Unlike boundaries, walls keep people out entirely. Walls hide us and help us avoid others. Unlike boundaries, which expand as our hearts transform, walls are nonnegotiable and trusted in place of the Comforter who lives in us.

We build emotional walls to protect our triggers. Rather than disarming the bomb and expanding the playground, we try to protect the explosive and limit the scope of life we can enjoy. We fight to keep people away from our triggers, trapping ourselves in a stifling prison of suspicion and vigilance, never letting our guard down for an instant.

If one of your big red buttons is strapped to a chair, you might be tempted to draw a wall around the chair. "You're not allowed to sit there because it triggers me." But chairs are for sitting in. Healthy relationships work both directions. Not only do we let people in, but we give them access to every appropriate place in our hearts. If your spouse sits on a button that's fixed to a chair, you don't have a spouse problem or a boundary problem; you have a trigger problem. More accurately, you don't even have a trigger problem; you have a bomb problem. People should be able to sit on chairs without triggering an explosion.

If the way your spouse is treating you is objectively appropriate but you find yourself triggered, recognize that a wound exists, and talk to your spouse about your sinful reaction. See if the two of you can prayerfully identify the source of the wound.

Triggers and Traumas

When I was a young teen, a lightbulb burned out in the lamp next to me. Taking initiative to change the bulb, I reached up to unscrew the old bulb and burned my fingers.

For years, whenever I had to change a lightbulb, I hesitated. I quickly tapped the old bulb to make sure it was safe to touch. It didn't matter that technology has advanced and all our lightbulbs are now LEDs that burn cool. My brain wouldn't let me grab a lightbulb without a twinge of anxiety.

This is the nature of a trauma response. It's your brain's way of protecting you from experiencing the same trauma again.

If the act of changing a lightbulb triggers me, should I therefore never change lightbulbs? Or should I recognize that changing a lightbulb is a safe, normal, and valuable behavior, and therefore, I should press past my anxiety and learn to trust lightbulbs again?

That is, in fact, what happened. Over time, I learned to trust light bulbs again. I have even reached up and unscrewed a lit LED bulb without thinking twice. By deliberately putting myself in situations that taught me to trust, I eventually overcame my anxiety.

Emotional and physical trauma work in much the same way. Around the same age as my lightbulb incident, I stayed the night at a relative's house. The couple was newly married and fought the whole time I was there. I was embarrassed to watch the way my relative's wife treated him. And by evening, the fighting escalated into a screaming match with the wife throwing objects and shouting swear words I had never heard in my young, sheltered life. I trembled in the guest bedroom, covering my ears and begging God to make it stop.

Later, when Robin and I were dating, I did something that offended her during a holiday gathering with her extended family. Naturally, Robin wanted to confront me and address the situation. But I felt a trauma response related to arguing in front of others. I wanted to escape the problem as quickly as possible. I apologized quickly, but that didn't satisfy Robin. She could tell I was avoiding the real issue and not fully understanding what I had done. I hurried out of the house, not wanting anyone present to experience the sort of trauma I had experienced as a kid. Robin followed me outside, fuming that I was dodging the issue instead of dealing with it.

"I don't want to fight in front of people!" I protested.

"What? You just want to pretend we never fight and that our lives are perfect? What are you afraid of? You think everyone believes we never argue?"

I paused for a moment. I didn't know exactly how to respond. "I just don't like making other people feel awkward."

"Well, now you've made *me* feel awkward. I feel like everyone inside knows we're out here having a fight, and now we have to go back in there and pretend like nothing happened. I don't know why you care more about everyone in the house than you do about me."

Not only was I triggered by fighting in front of people, Robin was triggered by my act of prioritizing a room full of people over her. We were playing ping-pong with each other's triggers, setting each other off more and more.

I actually don't remember how the rest of that conversation went—it has been about twenty years. But I do remember that it took me months to connect the dots between my present feelings and my earlier trauma at my relative's house. Until then, this was a constant battle for us. Because Robin felt insecure about whether I valued her more than others, she deliberately started fights in front of others. And because I still had a trauma response, I kept trying to shut down the discussions or escape. It was the anxious-avoidant snowball I mentioned in the previous chapter, and we couldn't seem to stop.

Disarming Triggers

One day, I was asking the Lord why I couldn't seem to stop hurting Robin when we had an argument. My experience at my relative's house came to mind.

When the Lord shows you the source of a trigger, two things need to happen to disarm it. Some of us have done one or the other, and we wonder why we still struggle with emotional reactions. Both of the following are necessary: (1) total forgiveness and (2) identifying lies and replacing them with truth. Both actions require repentance from our own sinful reactions to trauma, such as unforgiveness and sinful judgment. Here again, the cross is the answer.

Total forgiveness is multifaceted. It includes forgiving the person or persons who hurt you. It might include forgiving additional people for not protecting you. You may even need to forgive yourself for whatever role you played in the trauma. And even though God never did anything wrong, many people need to surrender the bitterness, anger, and resentment that they hold against him for letting the hurtful event take place.

As mentioned in chapter 5, forgiveness is impossible. We have to define our unforgiveness as sin, which means we can't conquer it ourselves and need to surrender it to the cross. Then, once we consider it dead with Christ, we can trust the Holy Spirit who lives in us to produce Jesus's forgiveness through us. We are then free to choose to forgive in the strength of the Lord.

Many Christians successfully forgive the people associated with their traumas, but they never deal with the lies they were taught in those experiences. Every trauma offers one or more lies on a silver platter. When we're communing with the Lord and aware of his voice, those lies are easy to reject. Our hunger for understanding is satisfied by his words of comfort and truth. But especially in childhood, if we're not anchored in the truth of God's voice to us, we'll probably receive and internalize the lies, adding them to the internal framework of our spiritual, emotional, and psychological operating system.

At my relative's house, a few lies were offered to me. First, I was taught that women aren't safe opponents in an argument. Second, arguing in front of others is traumatizing to them. And third, I'm powerless to stop someone's out-of-control emotion.

I believed all three lies to varying degrees. Thankfully, my mother was usually more level-headed in an argument, so the first lie wasn't accepted across the board. I took it more as a commentary on *some* women, but I had no way of knowing if Robin was one of those women since I never let our fights escalate. The other two lies, I embraced entirely.

But identifying and rejecting the lies is only half the battle. The other half is recognizing and receiving God's truth.

After I forgave my relative and his wife for their immaturity and violence and after I forgave my parents for putting me in that situation by sending me to my relative's house, I brought the lies to the Lord.

I prayed, "Lord, I reject the lie that women aren't safe opponents in an argument. What truth do you want me to know instead?"

The Lord spoke instantly. "Unsafe people are part of this fallen world, but you are safe because my Spirit lives in you."

Peace flooded my heart.

I continued, "I feel like it's not a lie that arguing in front of others is traumatizing because *I* was traumatized by it. Can you help me with this one?"

The Lord answered in my thoughts. "Arguing in front of others is only traumatizing when the way you argue is traumatizing. But I have given you and Robin self-control. Choose to argue with love and kindness, and no one will be traumatized. They will actually be helped."

"I feel the same way about my powerlessness to stop someone's out-of-control emotion. What do I do if the situation gets out of hand?"

"It's not your responsibility to control other people's actions. Exercise self-control, and give others the freedom to make their own right or wrong decisions. Your measured responses will expose their sinful actions and bring conviction."

By talking to the Lord about what the trauma taught me, my trauma was exposed as a false teacher, and the true Teacher discipled my heart in truth.

This is what Jesus promised us when he said, "I have much more to say to you, more than you can now bear. But when he, the Spirit of truth, comes, he will guide you into all the truth" (John 16:12–13). Trust the Holy Spirit to guide you into all the truth, and give him opportunities to counteract the lies this fallen world taught you.

If you will take the time to completely forgive all the people associated with your traumas, identify the lies learned, seek the Lord for truth, and truly believe what he reveals to you, you'll find the triggers no longer affect you, and you can expand the boundaries of your playground. I know that feels daunting—and perhaps even impossible. In some ways, it's a lifelong pursuit. But God is faithful, and he will do it (1 Thessalonians 5:23–24).

Opening Your Heart

Your spouse is a God-given bomb-detector to help you identify and address sinful triggers in your life. Sometimes, your spouse may be the only person in the world who triggers you in a particular way. Praise God for them, because that sin existed in your heart long before your spouse triggered you. You might never have known you were harboring lies or unforgiveness that offended the Lord if not for your spouse bringing it to the surface. Rather than being angry at your spouse and putting up walls, thank your spouse for bringing to light something you didn't know was in your heart.

Your spouse can then also be a blessing to you by being part of your quest for a solution. When I identify unforgiveness in my heart, I confess my sin to Robin, and she voices God's forgiveness to me in return. "You are forgiven in the name of Jesus." Because we're working through the issue together, she holds me accountable to expressing forgiveness out loud—not merely settling for a feeling in my heart but putting concrete words to it. "I choose to forgive [that person] for [that behavior]." And then, as someone who understands how this works, she asks, "What are the lies that experience taught you?" She listens as I process out loud. Then we pray, and she waits patiently while I listen for the Lord to speak truth into my heart. I then share the truth I learned, and we rejoice together.

You don't have to be afraid of your triggers. They simply expose sin that was there all along. And since we want to completely eradicate sin from our lives, our triggered responses are helpful. It's like a person experiencing a medical symptom like dizziness, and their doctor discovers a life-threatening heart problem. The dizziness, while uncomfortable, was helpful because it exposed a hidden problem. It's not that we celebrate when we sin; it's that we celebrate the exposure of sin so that we can render it dead on the cross.

In short, you don't need to protect your triggers from your spouse. Let your spouse come close enough to bump into those triggers, and then bring those issues to the cross. Soon, you'll discover much more on the playground of a healthy marriage than you ever knew was available. You and your spouse will begin to feel free.

Gathering Your Thoughts

Write down your thoughts about these questions before talking to your spouse about this chapter. Talk to the Lord about any shortcomings you see in yourself, and simply trust him to immediately bring forgiveness, freedom, and transformation to your heart.

1. Which of your spouse's behaviors tend to trigger you most often or most severely? What feelings rise in you when you're triggered? What pain or possible trauma are you trying to avoid or escape? When is the first time you remember experiencing that same feeling?
2. When considering the first time you experienced that pain or trauma, is there anyone you need to forgive? If so, remember that Jesus paid the price for that person's sin, and pray, "I choose to forgive [name] for [behavior]."
3. Next, ask the Lord what lie(s) that experience taught you. See what comes to mind. Then ask the Lord what truth he wants you to know that will counteract the lie. Write down whatever truth comes to mind.

Conversation Starters

Open up to your spouse about the following topics. Require nothing from them—only give.

1. Share what impacted you most about this chapter.
2. If you identified a trigger, a past trauma, and any lies in the above exercise, share your testimony with your spouse and ask them to help you discern whether any truths that came to mind sound like God's perspective.

Ask your spouse the following:

1. What behaviors of mine tend to trigger you the most?
2. How can I help you deescalate when you feel triggered?

CHAPTER 9:

Freedom from the Past

MY WIFE AND I WERE MARRIED THE SAME YEAR THAT MY parents retired and moved out of state. The blessing for my new bride and me was that my parents sold us their double-wide mobile home for only twenty thousand dollars.

My parents chose a retirement of full-time RVing, which meant they couldn't take much with them. They left behind their two-year-old king-size bedroom set, big-screen TV, all their furniture and appliances, and so much more. Robin and I were able to start our marriage with a tremendous head start.

My parents are resourceful and crafty, which means they saved almost every little scrap of wood or fabric. They are also both sentimental and tend to hold onto anything with a memory attached, even if it's otherwise worthless. They were never hoarders, but they did accumulate a lot of belongings over the decades. So along with the blessings my parents handed down with the house, Robin and I also received everything tucked into the back of every cupboard and closet, the junk drawer that every middle-class family seems to have, the two-story shed, and more.

We sold a few things and saved some for my own sentimental reasons. Others, we gave away to my siblings. And as for the rest, let's just say that during our first month of marriage, we put about thirty garbage bags on the curb each week.

We all inherit both good and bad from those who raised us. Many of us hold so tightly to the bad that we have no room for any good of our own. Robin and I couldn't even put away our wedding shower gifts until we created space for them. Likewise, it's hard to create new memories together when we're still living in the past.

Enjoying the Promise

Ephesians 6:2–3 teaches us, "'Honor your father and mother'—which is the first commandment with a promise—'so that it may go well with you and that you may enjoy long life on the earth.'" If you want a long life that goes well, Scripture tells us how. And that means the opposite is also true. If you want a short life that does not go well, then you can dishonor your parents. As Deuteronomy 27:16 notes, "Cursed is anyone who dishonors their father or mother."

In 2010, I interviewed John Loren Sandford (1929–2018), founder of Elijah House Ministries. He shared what he and his wife, Paula, had taught throughout the previous decades: "We have found this to be an absolute principle, that if you honor your father or mother, life *will* go well with you. But in every area where you could not or did not honor your father or mother, life will *not* go well with you. So it lies at the very basis of our life. The Lord came that we might have life abundantly, but when we have dishonor of our parents, then life cannot go abundantly."

He continued, pointing to Romans 2:1, which says, "You, therefore, have no excuse, you who pass judgment on someone else, for at whatever point you judge another, you are condemning yourself, because you who pass judgment do the same things."

Naturally, it's possible that we don't do the same things as what we judge in others. But, in Isaiah 55:11, God said, "My word that goes out from my mouth . . . will not return to me empty, but will accomplish what I desire and achieve the purpose for which I sent it." Or you might be familiar with the older language: "It shall not return to me void" (NKJV). In other words, God's words will not be without effect. So as John Loren Sandford pointed out, if we're not presently guilty of the same things we judge in others, we soon will be. The Scripture will be proven true.

It's worth clarifying that not all judgment is bad. There's a difference between righteous judgment and sinful judgment. Righteous judgment is exercised by Christians regarding other Christians (1 Corinthians 5:12–13). Righteous judgment is based on truth and aligns with God's view of a matter (Romans 2:2). It is for the purpose of rescuing unrepentant Christians from sinful ruts that threaten their eternity (1 Corinthians 5:4–5).

Sinful judgment, on the other hand, forms conclusions about people according to our own subjective feelings and has no hope attached.

When we sinfully judge our parents, both of these spiritual principles begin working against us. Not only does life not go well for us, but we even find ourselves doing the same sorts of things. And this can affect us for decades until we surrender our sinful judgments to the cross and align our hearts with God's truth.

For example, in my interview, eighty-year-old John said, "Just today, I was dealing with that very thing . . . . I judged my mother for foolish, selfish spending, and I just realized today that some of my foolish, selfish spending comes from exactly that. I judged her, so I did the same thing. I've taught this material for fifty years, I've gone through hundreds of prayer sessions, and here the Lord drags up another one!"

Over the decades, as pastors and with countless counseling clients, John and Paula observed these consistent and inescapable principles. And I have experienced fruit in this teaching for my own life and ministry to many others as well.

If someone's life is not going well with them, the first place we look is their experiences (or lack thereof) with their mom and dad. God wants you to enjoy this promise, but it comes with a stipulation: honor your parents.

This doesn't mean that your parents need to be particularly honorable people. You're not responsible for whether they're honorable; you're responsible for whether you honor them. This can look like being honest about their shortcomings while also viewing them with compassion or being honest about the struggles they endured that led them down that sinful road. Or like Noah's two sons, you can choose to cover your parents' shame rather than exposing it (Genesis 9:20–23). "Love covers over a multitude of sins" (1 Peter 4:8).

Certainly, we do not excuse abuse or avoid reporting criminal behavior to the appropriate authorities. And there is still a place for meekly but firmly confronting sin when it will benefit our parents (1 Timothy 5:1). Love and honor do not excuse or ignore sin, but they do cover shame. Rather than railing against your parents, complaining about their failures, or using their behaviors to excuse your present sins, you can forgive, lovingly confront as needed, and move on in victory.

When Robin and I were dating, her parents requested that she finish college before we tied the knot. We dated for seven years. And as a couple of well-raised church kids who were saving our virginity for marriage, those seven years were not easy! But we powered through in the strength of the Lord and honored her parents' wishes.

I have no idea about all the ramifications that this has had on our lives, but I can certainly say that our decision to honor Robin's parents aligned the timing of our wedding with my own parents' retirement, resulting in the tremendous head start we received when they sold us their house and gave us all their belongings. The impact of our decision to honor them is still being felt fifteen years later.

Perhaps you regret past decisions and the opportunities lost. Don't worry. The Lord is merciful. When you repent, he takes the ramifications of your sin at the cross. His blood cleanses you. He reaps the evil you sowed so that you can reap the righteousness he sowed. The Lord can turn any situation around so the rest of your life can go well with you.

Simply surrender unforgiveness, anger, resentment, and sinful judgments to the cross by confessing them to a fellow believer— perhaps even your spouse. Then, let the Lord speak to your heart about how he sees your parents. Recalibrate your heart to God's truth and righteous judgment. Then love and honor your parents moving forward.

Sowing and Reaping

In their writing, the Sandfords point out another biblical principle from Hebrews 12:15. "See to it that no one falls short of the grace of God and that no bitter root grows up to cause trouble and defile many." They demonstrate that the bitter, sinful thoughts and attitudes in our hearts, when left unchecked, soon defile other people.[29]

This happens in some obvious ways. We've already talked about triggers and the pent-up energy we unleash on others. One could say that's the defilement that affects others. But a less obvious mechanism is also at work: sowing and reaping.

Galatians 6:7–8 says, "Do not be deceived: God cannot be mocked. A man reaps what he sows. Whoever sows to please their flesh, from the flesh will reap destruction; whoever sows to please the Spirit, from the Spirit will reap eternal life." Sowing and reaping—planting and harvesting—are real spiritual principles that transpire every day. Our actions influence future experiences, for better or worse.

How do we reap? Certainly, we experience natural consequences all the time. But sometimes God goes beyond the natural order to bring correction. Isaiah 63:10 says, "Yet they rebelled and grieved his Holy Spirit. So he turned and became their enemy and he himself fought against them." Sometimes what we reap is God's discipline to us as dearly loved children (Hebrews 12:5–11).

Many times in Israel's history, God turned human enemies against his people to discipline them. For example, after God set Israel free from Egypt and brought them into the promised land, Israel largely continued serving idols for roughly one thousand years. Finally, God brought judgment by giving over Israel to Babylon (Isaiah 47:6). The Israelites sowed in idolatry and disobedience, and the Babylonians became the agents of Israel's reaping. One could say that the Babylonians were defiled by Israel's sin—swept into the mess to become the means by which Israel reaped what they were due.

Nevertheless, Babylon was held accountable for their actions against Israel (Jeremiah 50–51). God didn't make Babylon sin, as though they had no choice. But God did remove his protection from Israel and create a path for the Babylonian king to carry out the evil that was already in his heart. Even when someone becomes

---

[29] John Loren and Paula Sandford, *Transforming the Inner Man*, (Lake Mary, Florida: Charisma Media/Charisma House Book Group, 2007), 145–178.

God's tool for our reaping, they are still accountable to God for their own actions.

I like to think of this principle like a river, flowing in the direction of the person who sowed in sin—a spiritual flow meant to invite or facilitate the reaping that our actions called for. The degree to which someone is given over to their flesh, not exercising self-control, is the same degree to which they will be swept along in the direction of that spiritual flow.

Some friends, family, or strangers might stand only ankle deep in those waters. They stand firm, unmoved. They feel the current, tempting them to treat us a particular way, but they resist the urge.

Others, however, are so lost in sin or so wrapped up in the sinful desires of their flesh that they find themselves swept along in the river, treating us exactly as we deserve. Our bitter condition defiles those people, drawing them into sinful actions against us. Those who live by the Spirit and not the flesh will resist. But like the Babylonian king who became the means of Israel's reaping, those who live in their own strength are highly likely to sin in the very direction the river is flowing. The sin we sow demands reaping, and apart from faith in the cross of Christ, we are left to reap in the very ways we sowed—often through the hands of other sinful people who are being defiled by the spiritual influence of our bitterness.

Robin grew up in a home where people took initiative and finished what they started. Her parents' home was always clean. Dishes didn't sit in the sink for more than a few minutes. Her parents raised her to be conscientious and thoughtful of those around her. Everyone did their part and took responsibility. My family, on the other hand, loved to play. If the weather was nice, the chores could wait for rain. We also finished what we started, but only on our own terms. My dad's ongoing joke of a motto was *mañana* (the Spanish word for "tomorrow"), applying it whenever someone asked when we would get to a certain task. We regularly put off projects so we could enjoy the present. This was most visibly seen in our garbage can, which was often only emptied after the trash had piled twice as high as the can, requiring a second bag to be forced over the top.

Robin's and my families had similar values. Both worked hard and played hard. Both valued others. But the cultures of our homes followed two different sets of priorities for expressing those values. Neither was objectively right or wrong—just different.

When Robin and I were married, I expected her upbringing to be sufficient to keep our house clean. But I had sinfully judged my parents for so often prioritizing play over work. That law of sowing and reaping went into effect, and Robin found herself swept up in a spiritual river that rushed in the direction of procrastination. The bitter judgments in my heart had been sown, and spiritual law went to work to ensure that I reaped. Robin was defiled by my bitterness. Soon, we had a mountain of dirty laundry, a pile of dishes in the sink, clutter on every horizontal surface in the house, and a stack of garbage twice as tall as our can.

I was frustrated. I married someone with principles. Why couldn't we seem to manage our home?

The sinful judgment I held against my parents was poured back in my own direction. In Matthew 7:1–2, Jesus said, "Do not judge, or you too will be judged. For in the same way you judge others, you will be judged, and with the measure you use, it will be measured to you." I was reaping what I had sown, and Robin was being defiled to become the one through whom I reaped.

The Lord prompted my heart, and I had a revelation. I said, "Honey, I think we're dealing with something spiritual here. I even think a spirit of procrastination might be in our home. I don't know. I just know that while this lifestyle has been normal for me throughout my life, this isn't normal for you, and I think spiritual forces are working against us both." I repented of sinfully judging my parents and commanded any unclean spirit to leave our home.

Robin asked, "What do you think we should do?"

I said, "The laundry."

That day, everything turned around for us. We cleaned our whole house. Since then, we maintain what feels like a healthy balance between keeping our home tidy and not being ruled by it. Dishes can sit in our sink overnight without bothering us, but our house is generally presentable. Little bits of clutter can be found here and there, but we tidy them up as we have the opportunity.

The river has turned around. Or, rather, *I* turned around. My repentance sent all my reaping to the cross so that we could reap from the righteous life Jesus sowed.

This is just one of many examples where Robin and I have forgiven our wonderful parents for their moments of flesh, repented of our sinful judgments of them and others, and chosen to believe God's thoughts about the many valuable people in our lives. We now find ourselves in a river of blessing, no longer defiled by each other's bitterness. We can easily move in the right direction as we both walk in the life of the Spirit, unhindered by bitterness from the past.

The Power of the Cross

Sowing and reaping is a real spiritual principle, but we need to understand it in the light of the cross. Jesus did not come to make sure we all reap what we've sown. That's what would have happened if he *didn't* come.

At the cross, a supernatural exchange took place in which Jesus reaped everything we have sown so that we could reap everything he has sown. He took all the pain and punishment for our sin that we deserved. And in its place, he offers us union with himself, enabling us to enjoy the eternal, abundant life that only he deserves. In 2 Corinthians 1:20, we see that "no matter how many promises God has made, they are 'Yes' in Christ."

No matter how much sin you have sown in the past, Jesus's blood is enough to overcome it. No matter how massive our sins against God, his grace grows to meet the need and conquer it (Romans 5:20–21). We can truly think of our old lives as having died with Jesus so that we can now live in the new way of the Holy Spirit (Romans 6:11; 7:6).

No husband will be excused at the judgment by saying, "Lord, if it hadn't been for all my wife's bitterness, I would have been a better person. She's the reason I didn't obey you." Adam tried blaming his own disobedience on his wife, but God didn't let him off the hook (Genesis 3:12). This tells me that no one is doomed to be the product of their spouse's bitterness. God can make us stand firm in Christ, never stumbling (2 Corinthians 1:21; Jude 1:24).

If you put all of your confidence in Jesus's sacrifice and believe that his Spirit who lives in you can help you express God's victorious nature, then you don't have to worry about what bitterness might be lurking under the surface in your spouse. You simply need to make sure that you have thoroughly crucified every bitter root in your own life, living by the Spirit and not the sinful judgments, resentments, and wounds of the past. The objective is not to change your spouse but to be transformed. Nevertheless, as you are transformed, you might find that your spouse's behavior begins to change as well.

Trusting Jesus's Victory

Yet another problem that our past offers us is our tendency to fight sinful patterns with personal resolve. We might say, "I'll never treat my kids the way my parents treated me." Then, when we later have kids, we find ourselves doing the exact things we swore we wouldn't do.

In these cases, not only are we fighting the biblical principles already mentioned, but yet another layer of pride exists. Only an arrogant heart is bold enough to declare, "I will never . . ." with such certainty. The Bible warns us that "pride goes before destruction, a haughty spirit before a fall" (Proverbs 16:18). And "God opposes the proud but shows favor to the humble" (James 4:6).

It takes tremendous pride to look at a sin that someone else failed to overcome and assume that we're somehow stronger than them. In the late 1800s, the famous evangelist Dwight L. Moody is said to have been walking down the street with a friend. A drunken man staggered toward them on the street and soon stumbled into the gutter. As Moody's friend pondered his own ideas about the man, Rev. Moody quietly stated, "There, but for the grace of God, goes Dwight Moody."[30] Brother Moody knew that if not for God's sustaining grace, he could easily fall into the same situation.

As soon as we say, "I will always" or "I will never," we position ourselves for defeat. God opposes us. It's like he says,

---

[30] "There—But for the Grace of God—Goes Dwight Moody," Berkeley Daily Gazette, Berkeley, California, March 4, 1937, https://news.google.com/newspapers?id=JRkyAAAAIBAJ&sjid=nuMFAAAAIBAJ& pg=2370%2C399434.

"You think you can do that without grace? Watch what you can do without grace." Suddenly, we find ourselves incapable of behaving according to our will.

Contrast this with the position the apostle Paul took in 2 Corinthians 12:9–10. "Therefore I will boast all the more gladly about my weaknesses, so that Christ's power may rest on me. That is why, for Christ's sake, I delight in weaknesses, in insults, in hardships, in persecutions, in difficulties. For when I am weak, then I am strong."

In the first part of verse 9, God said to Paul, "My grace is sufficient for you, for my power is made perfect in weakness." When Paul realized his own inability to produce victory with his own strength, God was happy to go to work through him. God gave grace to his humble son.

Rather than saying, "I will never treat my spouse the way my parents treated each other," a better statement would be, "Jesus will never treat my spouse in that way." Since "I no longer live, but Christ lives in me," I can trust him to be himself through me (Galatians 2:20). I don't have to worry about whether I will be a good husband or a good father because Jesus lives in me, and he is perfect.

If you see unhealthy patterns in your marriage that remind you of ways your parents treated each other, you're probably experiencing the fruit of spiritual principles working against you. This is actually beneficial because it helps you identify sin that God wants removed from your heart so that you can be made more and more into his image and likeness. Bring it to the Lord and talk to him about it.

If you need to forgive your parents, forgive them. If you need to surrender a lie, put it on the cross. If you need to repent of sinful judgments, confess them and ask God to teach you his perspective. And along with all that, crucify the pride that led you to believe that you could live any differently in your own strength.

Be Proactive

While a certain amount of this transformation can happen passively as God reveals truth to us over time, my greatest growth happened when I started actively asking the Lord to expose and correct anything in my heart that didn't align with the nature of

Jesus. Like King David, I prayed, "Search me, God, and know my heart; test me and know my anxious thoughts. See if there is any offensive way in me, and lead me in the way everlasting" (Psalm 139:23–24).

I also invited scrutiny from my wife. It probably wouldn't have gone as well if she had imposed her critiques without my invitation, but I granted her permission. I said, "I want to be like Jesus and treat you like Jesus. So if you see anything in me that doesn't look like him, I want you to point it out to me." Taking my lead, Robin made the same request of me. It was a risky invitation, and it led to some tense moments for both of us, but it was also transformational.

Robin and I have made a habit of honoring this request every time something comes to the surface that doesn't look like Jesus. In the beginning, it seemed to be almost daily, which was annoying. But in time, the incidents became less frequent. We started demonstrating Jesus to each other for longer periods—not by our own effort but resting in the strength of the Holy Spirit.

We became quite adept at identifying when our present behaviors were rooted in past problems. Once, we were driving home from a family gathering. Robin was in tears because of something someone had said to her. I could see plainly that this was the fruit of a childhood wound, but I knew she needed compassion from me first before she could work through her emotions with any sense of rationality.

One of the best things you can do for your spouse when they're spiraling emotionally is provide emotional scaffolding for them. Scaffolding is a stable structure built around a project that may not yet be stable on its own. In other words, be a strong and measured presence that makes your spouse feel safe as they're processing their emotions. For a few minutes, set aside your own offenses, fears, and frustrations. Give your spouse a calm presence that helps them find stability.

I listened to Robin's complaint, and when it was clear to me that she felt loved and knew I had heard her, I gently asked, "Do you mind if I make an observation?"

Robin emotionally fired back, "Don't you dare say that this is all coming from some childhood wound and I need to forgive that person."

I couldn't help but chuckle. I bit my lip with a sheepish smile as an awkward tension filled the quiet car.

"Ugh!" she groaned. "You're right. Okay. Let's do this."

By being lovingly proactive about each other's transformation in this way, Robin and I have experienced a deep work in our hearts. We're more like Jesus today because we have systematically removed every hidden motivation in our hearts that has surfaced over the years.

Are there still more? Probably, but the Lord isn't highlighting those to us right now. Like the apostle Paul, we can say, "My conscience is clear, but that does not make me innocent" (1 Corinthians 4:4). The Lord is patient with us and doesn't bring up our issues until he knows it's time to deal with them. Accordingly, we can trust his wisdom, knowing that it is always God's perfect timing that we are addressing a matter of the heart. We don't need to protest that we're not ready. If the Lord is bringing it up, he is ready, and he loves us.

"As God's co-workers we urge you not to receive God's grace in vain. For he says, 'In the time of my favor I heard you, and in the day of salvation I helped you.' I tell you, now is the time of God's favor, now is the day of salvation" (2 Corinthians 6:1–2). Welcome the Lord's work in you. It's always the right time to be set free.

Gathering Your Thoughts

Write down your thoughts about these questions before talking to your spouse about this chapter. Talk to the Lord about any shortcomings you see in yourself, and simply trust him to immediately bring forgiveness, freedom, and transformation to your heart.

1. Ask the Lord if you have dishonored your parents in any way. If so, forgive them for their shortcomings, and receive the Lord's forgiveness for any sinful thoughts or actions you have identified.
2. Ask the Lord if there is anyone you are sinfully judging. If so, ask God to give you his thoughts about the person. Confess your sinful judgments to the Lord and receive forgiveness and freedom as you align your heart with God's truth.
3. Ask the Lord if you have made any prideful statements that have positioned you to be opposed by God rather than empowered by his grace. If so, surrender that independence to the cross, ask God for help, and express to him your trust in his empowerment.

Conversation Starters

Open up to your spouse about the following topics. Require nothing from them—only give.

1. Share what impacted you most about this chapter.
2. If the Lord showed you any sinful thoughts, attitudes, or actions in the above exercise, confess them to your spouse, and apologize for any ways your bitterness might have defiled them.
3. Invite your spouse to confront you when sin is obvious. Ask them to help you see when you're treating them in ways that are inconsistent with the nature of Jesus.

Ask your spouse the following:

1. Is there any way I have been treating you recently in which I seem to be unaware that I'm hurting you rather than helping?

CHAPTER 10:

Holy Conflict

JIM AND SARAH SAT ON OPPOSITE SIDES OF MY LIVING ROOM. They had been married for only a couple of years, and they were already considering a divorce.

Jim was most upset by Sarah's continued communication with her former boyfriend. She and the other man had a child together when they were young, so she felt a certain obligation to maintain relationship, even though the child had been adopted by another family. Jim struggled to articulate the hurt he felt when she would sit at home texting her ex instead of engaging with him. In moments of anger, she had even stoked the fires of insecurity by comparing the two men and talking about what she liked more about her former love interest.

Jim asked me, "Didn't Jesus say that to lust after someone is the same as adultery? Doesn't that mean I have the right to divorce her?"

I answered, "Well, let's be clear about the context. When Jesus said those words, he was raising the bar on lust, not lowering the bar on divorce. Divorce is a serious matter."

I read a number of Scriptures about divorce. Among them was Malachi 2:16, which says, "'The man who hates and divorces his wife,' says the Lord, the God of Israel, 'does violence to the one he should protect,' says the Lord Almighty. So be on your guard, and do not be unfaithful." In Matthew 19:8, Jesus declared, "Moses permitted you to divorce your wives because your hearts were hard. But it was not this way from the beginning."

I told him, "Divorce happens because of hardness of heart, not because God prefers it. Given the situation as I currently understand it, if you divorce your wife right now, you will be doing violence to her and demonstrating your own hardness of heart."

Some might disagree with my decision to steer this troubled couple away from divorce. Many would have advised something like, "You don't need to put up with this, Jim. Get out now before you subject yourself to more unnecessary pain. You're worth more than how she's treating you." If they were only dating, that might be sound advice. But remember that marriage is not like most relationships. It's a covenant. Consider God's covenant with you, which is perfect even when you're broken and unfaithful to him. Imagine if someone counseled God about covenant the way we counsel each other when a marriage is struggling.

Is Conflict Ever Too Severe?

I also talked to them about appropriate grounds for divorce. Jesus and Paul both presented reasons that God would permit divorce. Jesus cited sexual immorality (Matthew 19:9). Paul cited abandonment by an unbelieving spouse (1 Corinthians 7:15). If these were the only reasonable grounds for divorce, then they would have been stated together both times. Instead, they are presented in isolation by two different people in two different New Testament books, leaving open the possibility that other valid reasons may exist.

In Exodus 21:10–11, a woman given to a man's son as a wife is free to leave if the young man deprives her of "food, clothing, and marital rights." In 1 Corinthians 7, Paul mentions these same three concepts, commanding spouses not to deny marital rights (vv. 2–5), not to abandon or neglect each other (vv. 10–16), and to care for each other's needs (vv. 32–35). Accordingly, some have made the case—and I agree—that abuse and neglect are also within the bounds of Scripture as valid reasons for divorce.[31] The warning issued in Malachi 2:16 connects divorce to violence, proving that God hates the violent treatment of one's spouse.

---

[31] Joshua Sharp, "Voices: Abuse is biblical grounds for divorce," Baptist Standard, May 18, 2020, https://www.baptiststandard.com/opinion/voices/abuse-is-biblical-grounds-for-divorce/.

If you are reading this book and experiencing abuse, find safety immediately. If your spouse has broken the law with domestic violence, it is right, appropriate, and necessary to call the police and file a report as soon as possible. You do not need to protect your abuser from the consequences of their actions; in fact, the opposite is true. Make sure you and any children are safe. God can work amazing miracles in any situation, but do not put yourself in harm's way. Don't try to keep up appearances or guard an abuser's reputation. Seek help, and be honest about your situation so that your spouse can receive the intervention they need.

Also, if you are physically safe but feel emotionally unsafe with your spouse and find that the two of you are volatile when together, you may want to consider a temporary separation while the two of you work on your own relationships with the Lord first. This may require one of you to live in a separate room of the house or a separate home altogether. Your pastor may be able to help arrange a temporary roommate for one of you so it's not too much of a burden to your finances. Many times, people need to separate in order to give the fight-or-flight mechanism in their brains time to calm down enough for them to think clearly. Never be ashamed of doing what you have to do to heal your most important human relationship. Talk to a trustworthy Christian mentor, pastor, or counselor who can help you consider an ideal next step.

I told the couple, "As far as I know, no one has actually committed adultery, no one has left, and no one is being abused. At this point, I believe it's better for us to focus on repairing the broken trust."

I turned to Sarah. "It looks like you're going to need to decide who you're married to. Is it Jim or your ex? Only one of them has spoken vows to you."

Sarah then dropped a bombshell that I was not prepared to navigate. "What about Kelly?" (She was a friend of Sarah's.)

"Huh?" Jim's face flushed as he turned to look at her.

"You fell asleep with your phone open on your chest, and I saw your conversation. Did you sleep with her?"

Jim hung his head in shame.

He had.

Taking a breath to compose myself in the light of such unexpected news, I turned to Sarah. "Well, it looks like *you* have biblical grounds to divorce Jim. So you really do get to decide who you want to be married to."

I recommended that Jim stay with his parents for the weekend and give Sarah some time to process her feelings. We would all meet again in two days to discuss what she wanted to do.

Astoundingly, Sarah decided to forgive Jim. Both of them repented and ended their inappropriate and compromising relationships.

About a year later, Jim and Sarah were back in my living room with a new problem. They learned that when Jim engaged in his illicit affair, he contracted a sexually transmitted disease (STD), but it had not yet been passed to Sarah.

"What should I do?" Sarah asked.

The best answer I could offer her in the moment was, "Well, you did already forgive him. I don't want to play lawyer with the Bible, but I suppose you technically still have grounds for divorce if that's the path you want to take. I guess this leaves you with two options: option one, you divorce him, or option two, you stay married and choose to have an STD."

Today, more than five years later, Jim and Sarah are still together. Sarah demonstrated the gospel to Jim, offering mercy that was entirely undeserved. Her actions were transformative for both of them. When they gave me permission to share their story here, Sarah said, "I think it's a great testimony of how God can help you overcome even the most difficult of circumstances." I'm incredibly proud of both of them—not because everything is going perfectly in their lives but because every time they hit a rough patch, they both show up to work through their struggles. Their resilience and perseverance are evidence of God's grace at work.

Sometimes a situation is such that God permits divorce, but that doesn't mean God can't work with a couple who is open to his help. Make sure you're safe, try choosing hope, and look for wise counsel from someone who will help fight for your marriage.

Your Spouse Is Not Your Enemy

Robin and I have a peaceful home, but that's not because we always agree. In fifteen years of marriage, we've come to agree on several contentious points, but we've still maintained a few disagreements for over a decade. (I'm right, by the way.)

The Bible promotes unity among believers, but many have misunderstood what real unity looks like. For roughly a thousand years after Jesus ascended, despite various disagreements, all the churches in the known world saw themselves as one unified body.[32] Then controversy arose between the eastern and western churches over the authority of the Roman pope, whether priests should marry, the language of the Nicene Creed, and a few other matters, resulting in a divided church. About a half millennia later, Martin Luther protested the manipulation of Christians through a misuse of the church's power. This sent shockwaves through the Western church and resulted in the Protestant Reformation—yet another split among professing Christians.[33] Somewhere along the lines, Christians started parting ways over less and less important issues, so that today, there are roughly 45,000 Christian denominations around the world.[34]

A look at the New Testament will demonstrate that God cares far more about *how* we disagree than *that* we disagree. Love, humility, honor, gentleness, meekness, patience, and mutual dedication to the truth are vital among Christians, and these traits are essential to unity. Scripture warns us not to even bother arguing about certain minor issues (Titus 3:9–11; 2 Timothy 2:23). Biblical unity has less to do with everyone believing exactly the same doctrinal details (although major issues matter) and more to do with the love we express as we interact around those ideas.

Our divided church today has generally offered a poor example to believers of how to manage conflict. Rather than choosing commitment to one another and pursuing truth together no matter how long it takes, we cut and run. Those who don't like the new color of the carpet simply leave their church to find another congregation that better suits their preferences. And unfortunately, this culture has even seeped into many marriages.

---

[32] Timothy Paul Jones, PhD, *Christian History Made Easy*, (Carson, California: Rose Publishing, 2009), 69.

[33] John Hunt, *Concise Church History*, (Chattanooga, Tennessee: AMG Publishers, 2008), 283–301.

[34] Center for the Study of Global Christianity, Gordon-Conwell Theological Seminary, "Status of Global Christianity, 2024, in the Context of 1900–2050," https://www.gordonconwell.edu/wp-content/uploads/sites/13/2024/01/Status-of-Global-Christianity-2024.pdf.

All couples will disagree to one degree or another on matters of finance, parenting, intimacy, career choices, and more. The problem is not that we disagree but *how* we disagree.

Your spouse is not your enemy. "For our struggle is not against flesh and blood," Paul warns us (Ephesians 6:12). That means, if it has flesh and blood, you're not fighting it. Last I checked, every husband and every wife I've ever known was made of flesh and blood. Paul finished the verse, explaining that our struggle is "against the rulers, against the authorities, against the powers of this dark world and against the spiritual forces of evil in the heavenly realms."

You and your spouse are on the same team, fighting a shared enemy. That enemy wants to influence how you and your spouse disagree.

As Christians, we're invited to walk in victory over such spiritual forces. Paul spoke in the past tense, saying that the ways we "used to live" were influenced by "the ruler of the kingdom of the air, the spirit who is now at work in those who are disobedient" (Ephesians 2:2). Everyone has a spirit at work in them. If you're living in disobedience, it's not the Holy Spirit; he's holy. Therefore, if the ways we disagree look like disobedience to God, we're succumbing to our spiritual enemy rather than standing in victory over it.

Instead of a civil debate between two people who love each other, this spirit tempts one or both parties to elevate the dispute to what feels like a matter of life or death. Fight-or-flight kicks in, and rational thinking goes out the window. Emotions fly, tempers flare, and soon we are saying and doing things that feel entirely outside our control.

Soon, that spirit might even tempt one or both parties to start looking elsewhere for a different partner who already agrees with them. Like churches splitting or congregants jumping from one church to another, we selfishly search for the path of least resistance. It's easier than committing to each other for the long haul and figuring out how to walk in love and unity despite our disagreements. Marriages split, families are shattered, and the former spouses walk away feeling that their painful decision was entirely justified. All the while, our actual enemy is laughing at us and hanging the divorce papers on his hellish mantle as a trophy.

The enemy loves to bring division. He does it to churches, to friends, to families, and to marriages. And he does it by stoking the fires of selfishness that burn in individual hearts.

Leveraging Conflict

Many of us are terrified of conflict. We avoid it at all costs. But the absence of conflict is evidence that our relationship is superficial. Anytime two rivers merge into one, there are rapids for a time. Conflict is the natural result of two lives becoming one, but it ought not result in division.

Conflict is healthy for our spiritual and emotional development. It alerts us to sins and wounds we didn't know we carried. It creates an opportunity to seek God for wisdom and forces authenticity when it has been withheld. Conflict, when overcome, creates healthy bonds and stronger relationships.

Every time you and your spouse work through a conflict, your relationship strengthens. When you can anticipate the deeper friendship and truer intimacy that await on the other side of conflict, the pain of the journey becomes more tolerable.

People generally avoid conflict because they lack hope. If you don't expect a positive outcome, why would you even try to resolve the issue?

Sometimes this lack of hope manifests in a lack of trust in the other person. We trust ourselves, but we don't have any hope that the other person will be rational or reasonable. This might be true. But attempting to resolve the issue—if managed in a healthy way—is more likely to bring lasting benefit than cause worse problems. Even if the person isn't trustworthy, choose to have hope that God will work things together for your good as you seek peace and confront issues that need to be addressed (Romans 8:28).

When we avoid conflict, emotional tensions build. Resentment sets in. We might even take out our frustrations on other people. Soon, our relationship is plagued with discontentment and bitterness. We search for love and affirmation from friends, gossiping and complaining to people who can't do anything about our struggle. Meanwhile, the changes that need to happen remain unaddressed. And worst of all, what we're really avoiding is an opportunity to experience a deeper relationship.

If you truly want a healthy relationship, you'll need to engage in conflict, but you must do so in a healthy way.

Overcoming Obstacles to Healthy Conflict

The last three chapters have been devoted to topics that significantly affect how we behave during conflict. Triggers, attachment issues, and sinful mindsets can send us into behaviors that are out of bounds in a healthy, loving relationship. Certainly, the advice given in those chapters is vital for arguing in a way that honors God and each other.

Understanding your spouse's motivations can be helpful too. Even if you feel like they hate you, they might just be insecure and afraid, employing defense mechanisms that are hurtful but not actually personal. The way they're treating you may actually be the way they're lashing out at their mom or dad in their heart. This doesn't excuse their behavior, but it does help you not to internalize their words or actions.

Trust the Holy Spirit to produce Jesus's mercy and patience in you. Try to fully understand your spouse's perspective before informing them of your own perspective. The more your spouse feels heard, the more their emotions are likely to deescalate.

A lot of the emotion your spouse feels in a conflict is unresolved childhood trauma. For many, a fear of abuse or abandonment may spark a powerful fear reaction during a disagreement. By affirming your love and commitment to the person, you can help alleviate some of those insecurities before they spiral out of control.

How you choose to view your spouse matters. Value them. Believe the best about them. If you have already defined your spouse by their worst qualities, you'll interpret everything else they say or do through that lens.

You can identify if you're looking through a skewed lens if you use words like *always* or *never* when describing them. Such absolute words are unhelpful and put people on the defensive. They can undermine the validity of our intended point with even one example to the contrary.

Besides that, when we say things like, "You're always so hurtful," or "You never compliment me," we force the other person into a situation where they might begin striving in their flesh to prove us wrong, and that's sin.

Instead, we can confront their sin in a way that calls out the best in them. Imagine how you would feel if the way your spouse confronted your sin sounded like, "I know who you are. Jesus lives in you. He is kind, so I know you're a kind person. I've seen it in you. What you just did wasn't from Jesus. That's not who you are. Let's fight this together."

When you crucify your rights and exercise self-control from the Holy Spirit, you will find stability in conflict, even if the other person is doing the opposite. It's an act of self-sacrificial love to choose tenderness, gentleness, and mercy. And perhaps most importantly, it reveals Jesus to your spouse. As we discussed in chapter 5, this creates an opportunity for your spouse to be transformed more into Jesus's image and likeness.

Either one of you can choose to be the first person to do the right thing. Either one of you can step back from the emotion of the moment, look to Jesus, and ask, "Who do you want to be in this situation?" Then, become what you behold of him and return to the conflict in his image and likeness. Don't wait for your spouse to do it first. Be the vessel through whom Jesus leads your marriage.

This sort of resolution generally looks like self-sacrifice. From time to time, when Robin and I cannot resolve a debate, I have said, "I still believe I'm right, or else this wouldn't be an argument. But because I love you, let's do it your way. If it works out, I'll apologize. And if it fails, I'll take responsibility for it. I won't rub it in your face." In this, Jesus is seen—the one who took responsibility for the ramifications of our failures and declared us innocent. I have never regretted resolving a dispute this way.

Finally, one of the best tools Robin and I have employed is to talk about our concerns and frustrations when everything is going great. It feels like the worst possible time because everyone is happy, and we don't want to upset the peace. But it is actually the best time, because no one is in survival mode or experiencing fight-or-flight. Never be afraid of ruining a good day with a difficult conversation. Simply ask, "Are you in a good spot emotionally for me to talk to you about something that is bothering me?" If they are, go for it. And if they're not, don't worry. You've lived with the issue this long; you can live with it a little longer. Simply ask when would be a better time.

Killing the Past

Sometimes conflict arises over memories of past experiences. Memory is subjective and easily skewed, but generally, an objective outside party can piece together a picture of what probably transpired by listening to multiple accounts. The truth is often somewhere in the middle.

However, I've been in various situations with married couples who both believed incompatible versions of events. No objective evidence existed to prove who was right and who was fabricating their story. There wasn't a way to arrive at objective truth on the matter, so peace wasn't going to come by proving one right.

But a solution is always available. Jesus said, "Whoever wants to be my disciple must deny themselves and take up their cross and follow me" (Matthew 16:24). Self-denial is a denial of our rights. Many of us need to crucify the right to be right.

Remember our discussion of Galatians 6:14 from chapter 8. The cross crucifies the world to me. In other words, I consider the world no longer an option. My past is no longer accessible to me as an excuse for my present behavior. I can't reach into the world system and find a rationale that will justify my poor decisions and attitudes. And second, the cross crucifies me to the world. That means I'm no longer available to the world system (or the spiritual forces at work in it) to be its puppet. I'm inaccessible. My past can't touch me. Evil spirits can't touch me. The cross sets me free in both directions—I cannot access the world, and the world cannot access me. I'm a new creation in a new kingdom.

If I'm living out of my past, it's only because the old me isn't yet fully dead, and I'm letting my past pains speak louder than Jesus's suffering at the cross.

But Scripture offers a better way: "Forgetting what is behind and straining toward what is ahead, I press on toward the goal to win the prize for which God has called me heavenward in Christ Jesus" (Philippians 3:13–14). Sometimes, the only way forward in an argument over what exactly happened in the past is to surrender the whole scenario to the Lord and press on as a free person.

Our flesh wants so desperately for justice to be done on our behalf that we will dig in our heels and fight to ensure that the person who wronged us admits what they did and pays for their actions. And we can look right and holy while we do it. We're standing for truth, after all. But this only exposes that we don't believe Jesus's sacrifice is sufficient justice. It's a faith problem. His blood was shed not only for your sin but also for your spouse's sin (1 John 2:2).

When we put our faith in the justice exercised at the cross, we no longer need the other person to concede to us before we can move on. It's no longer about whether I'm right or you're right. Jesus is right, and that's all that matters. It is possible to say, "I don't think we're going to see eye to eye on this, but I have decided it's more important to love you than to convince you of my belief. So I'm not going to argue this issue with you anymore. I care too much about you to let this stand between us."

Rethinking Love Languages

In 1992, author Gary Chapman's book *The Five Love Languages* hit bookshelves. It ended up spending 297 weeks on the *New York Times* bestseller list.[35] His book was even assigned reading for me when I was in Bible school.

Chapman's premise was that there are five basic ways in which humans express and experience love: (1) words of affirmation, (2) quality time, (3) gifts, (4) acts of service, and (5) physical touch.[36]

Occasionally, conflict arises in a marriage because one or both spouses may be trying to communicate love in ways that the other isn't receiving.

I like to joke that I have a love-hate relationship with the five love languages. The book is fantastic for reminding us that there are multiple ways to express love. But more recent studies have demonstrated that what people need is a balanced diet of various

---

[35] "Paperback Advice & Misc.," *The New York Times*, April 21, 2013, https://www.nytimes.com/books/best-sellers/2013/04/21/paperback-advice/.

[36] Gary Chapman, *The Five Love Languages*, (Chicago: Northfield Publishing, 1992, 1995), 119.

expressions of love, not a narrow application of a favorite type.[37]
On one hand, love is self-sacrificial, so it's great to set aside our
own agendas and love people according to their needs and desires.
But I have seen far too many people weaponize the five love
languages, telling their spouse why they don't feel loved by them
and demanding certain treatment.

Robin's most dominant love language is acts of service while
mine is words of affirmation. I would smother Robin with kind
words and compliments, and she would work hard around the
house, but both of us felt neglected.

I read Chapman's book as I was studying to become a pastor,
and I brought what I was learning to Robin. It led to some great
conversations and helped us understand some of what was going
on between us.

But I had a revelation that I didn't pick up from the book. I
said, "I think it's helpful to try to show love in more ways. But if
we don't experience one or more of these expressions as love,
there's probably a wound there. I don't think it's healthy for me to
reject your expressions of love just because they're not my favorite.
I want to get to the bottom of why I don't feel loved when you're
trying to show me love."

It sort of reversed the way I understood the book. I didn't try
to convince Robin to speak more words of affirmation. I crucified
my selfishness. I let my heart rest in the affirmation I receive from
Father God. And then I dealt with the wounds in my heart that
were keeping me from seeing all Robin's hard work as love.

For some people, physical touch communicates love. For
others, trauma earlier in life has made such interaction
uncomfortable and perhaps even triggering. A married couple who
loves each other might cater to that discomfort while trust is built,
but eventually the heart must be transformed so that physical touch
is experienced as love rather than attack.

You can't control how your spouse expresses love to you, but
you can control your own willingness to interpret their actions as
love. This requires selflessness, humility, and love on your part as
you choose to believe the best about your spouse. See that they

---

[37] Denis Storey, "Study Refutes Concept of Love Languages," Psychiatrist.com, January
23, 2024, https://www.psychiatrist.com/news/study-refutes-concept-of-love-languages/.

truly want to love you, and verbally thank them for the ways they go out of their way to love you, even if it's not your favorite way to be loved. Also, pay attention to the ways they love you and reciprocate in similar ways. They may be expressing love in the same ways they are most likely to perceive it.

The more you and your spouse recognize each other's diverse expressions of love, the more stability will be present in your relationship, greatly helping you both during conflict. The more you surrender your right to be offended, the fewer unhealthy conflicts you'll have. The more you deny yourself, take up your cross, and follow Jesus, the brighter he will shine in your marriage. Choose to reveal Jesus to each other, and watch your friendship grow.

Gathering Your Thoughts

Write down your thoughts about these questions before talking to your spouse about this chapter. Talk to the Lord about any shortcomings you see in yourself, and simply trust him to immediately bring forgiveness, freedom, and transformation to your heart.

1. What did conflict between your parents or other influential adults look like when you were growing up? Did their behaviors indicate emotional stability and a long-term outlook on relationships? Do you feel that what you observed has affected your own views on conflict and how?
2. Are there any present disputes between you and your spouse in which you need to crucify the past and surrender your right to be right? If so, write down a prayer of surrender to the Lord, and offer the conflict to the cross, considering the past issue dead and trusting God to move you both forward in love and newfound unity.
3. Are there any areas in which you have been avoiding conflict for unhealthy reasons? Of course, some hills are not worth dying on. Never feel bad choosing peace when appropriate. But if you need to address any looming conflict for the sake of peace, pray about how to lovingly approach your spouse about it.
4. Consider the five love languages: (1) words of affirmation, (2) quality time, (3) gifts, (4) acts of service, and (5) physical touch. Which of these seems to be your favorite way to give and receive love? Which seems to be your spouse's favorite way to give and receive love? Are there any love languages that you do not perceive as love? If so, ask the Lord why, and write down any thoughts that might come to mind.

Conversation Starters

Open up to your spouse about the following topics. Require nothing from them—only give.

1. Share what impacted you most about this chapter.
2. Are there are any ways that your spouse has been trying to communicate love but that you have been rejecting because

of wounds in your heart? If so, apologize for not recognizing their love and ask them to be patient with you as you're learning to receive their love in that way.

3. If you are presently in conflict with your spouse about something, tell your spouse that you don't consider them the enemy. Then, together, try to identify what your shared enemy is (not another person, but perhaps a particular vice, fear, or evil spiritual force that is standing against the unity of your marriage). Verbally commit to fight against that real enemy instead of your spouse.

Ask your spouse the following:

1. When do you most feel that I love you? What am I doing during those times?
2. What is something I can do during conflict to assure you that you're not my enemy?
3. Is there anything I need to stop doing that has been communicating that I'm against you instead of just trying to solve a problem?

CHAPTER 11

Interpretive Dance

O N MY FIRST TRIP TO UGANDA, MY KENYAN GUIDE, Wycliffe, and I were dropped off in a remote town on the side of the road. We called my Ugandan contact, Pastor Paul Basule, to pick us up and take us to the village where he lived. Then we waited.

Minutes turned into hours. The sky grew dark. No one was answering Pastor Paul's phone. Wycliffe and I became concerned that either something happened to Paul or we had been in contact with a scammer. The streets were swarming with people, and Wycliffe was on high alert for thieves.

Then, another possibility occurred to us. Maybe the public transport van had dropped us off in the wrong town. The only way to find out was to ask.

Wycliffe, a pastor, spoke eight languages. Unfortunately, none of those languages was Luganda or Lusoga—the two most common languages in this area. And we were in a remote region where English speakers were incredibly rare. Wycliffe tried in vain to communicate with any of the multitude passing us on the street, but no one understood any of his eight languages.

Suddenly, two little children ran up to me. Seeing my rare skin color, they assumed I spoke English and offered a loud, "Hello!"

My eyes widened as relief washed over me. I excitedly asked them, "Do you speak English?"

The kids both nodded.

In my desire not to confuse them or scare them away, I tried my hardest to use simple words. I avoided more complicated vocabulary like "city" or "town" and simply asked, "What do you call this place?"

As though scripted, both children replied in unison, smiling from ear to ear and throwing their hands up in jubilation, "Uganda!"

In hindsight, this miscommunication makes me laugh, but in the moment, Wycliffe and I were concerned for our lives. With some clarifying, we did find out that we had been dropped off in the wrong town—a town known for crime and prostitution. Thankfully, word finally reached Pastor Paul, and we were eventually rescued.

Language matters. Whenever we cross cultures, communication becomes more complicated. Wycliffe spoke eight languages, but that didn't make him any better at communicating in a town where no one spoke any of them. Then, when we finally found someone who spoke the same language, a poorly posed question brought a bold answer that wasn't at all helpful. We thought we were speaking the same language, but what I meant and what those children heard were not the same.

You and your spouse likely speak the same language, but you still come from two different families, which means two different cultures. Coming together and communicating can be a complicated chore, especially in the beginning.

My first trip to rural Uganda was thirteen years ago, and I've now been there eleven times. Over the years, I've picked up a lot of words and phrases in their tribal dialect, and the people receive my attempts at communication as love. I'm still not yet fluent in their language, but we communicate better now than ever before. And through that communication, we've been able to produce a lot of good fruit. Pastor Paul, his team, and I have together built an orphanage and school, started thirteen churches, trained nearly two thousand ministers, and seen thousands of salvations and miracles.

If you and your spouse will commit to identifying and understanding each other's languages, you can avoid a lot of unintended offense and frustration and work together as an effective team.

Certainly, many people marry someone from a foreign country who literally speaks a different language. This presents its own challenges. But while what I'm about to share may help multilingual families communicate better, I'm not talking here about actual languages. I'm talking about styles of communication.

Direct vs. Indirect

A couple of nights ago, my wife said, "I bought some Italian sausage, noodles, and pasta sauce for tonight."

I said, "Great!"

An hour later, Robin asked, "Why haven't you started yet on making dinner?"

"You never asked."

"Yeah, I did." Then, realizing what she had done, she joked, "Didn't you understand that when I told you what I bought, it meant you're supposed to do all the cooking tonight?"

One of the language barriers Robin and I have noticed over the years is direct vs. indirect communication. Whereas Robin might say, "I'm cold," I would be more likely to say, "Can you please toss me that blanket?" Robin speaks indirectly while I say what I mean.

Neither of our communication styles is necessarily right or wrong. In some cultures, direct communication like mine can be seen as rude and harsh. But my concrete thinking means Robin's subtle cues don't often connect.

We figured this out early in our marriage. In frustration, I would beg Robin, "What do you want?"

She would answer, "If I tell you, then it's not as meaningful. I need you to know what I need without me saying it."

It took some convincing, but I finally helped her see that I'm not a mind reader. Also, I really do want to show her love. I said, "If you tell me exactly what you want and I do it, it's because I love you and want to take care of you. If you send a million hints and I don't get it, I still love you and want to take care of you. I'm just too thick-headed to understand. Please, help me love you and just say what you mean."

As you can see from my pasta story from two nights ago, we haven't perfected this yet. But because we've talked about this communication barrier over the years, we can now laugh about it, not fight about it.

Logic vs. Emotion

We were newly married, and Robin and I were snuggled up together in bed. She said sweetly, "Can I always be married to you?"

Naturally, my theologically accurate pastor brain kicked into gear. I replied, "Well, Jesus said that in eternity, we won't be married anymore, but we can be married for as long as we're both living here."

Wrong answer. A playful fist thumped into my shoulder. "When I say something like that to you, I'm not looking for a technical answer. I know that answer too. Just say yes and enjoy the moment."

Over the years, I've learned to accommodate Robin's desire for emotional connection, prioritizing the feeling of the moment over my own penchant for analytical accuracy.

This most often shows up when Robin is venting frustration. I used to immediately go into troubleshooting or problem-solving, and Robin would become even more frustrated. "I don't want you to fix it," she would say, "I just want you to hold me."

I soon learned to ask, "What do you need from me right now? Do you just need me to be present, or do you want me to offer solutions?" And over the years, I've learned that Robin consistently wants emotional comfort first and will ask for solutions when she's ready.

In case it's not clear, I'm not describing here the difference between men and women. Even though statistics might lean in the direction of men preferring logic over emotion and vice versa, every couple is unique. This isn't advice about how you should necessarily manage your own relationship. It's advice about identifying whether you and your spouse have different priorities in your communication and then loving the other by learning to accommodate their needs. Each couple's solutions will be a little different, depending on their needs.

Meticulous vs. Intuitive

Imagine two people visit the same room. Upon exiting, one comments to the other, "Did you see how much dust was on the mantle? And their carpet had stains. I can't even believe I saw those things because the lights were so dim."

The other replies, "I missed all that, but I noticed it was a bit dingy."

One person sees the trees, and the other sees the forest. One person sees the details while the other takes in the whole picture. The first is meticulous while the second is intuitive.

Sometimes, these two people marry each other. It can be a tremendous strength when the difference is recognized and valued. But it can also sometimes lead to unnecessary conflict.

Occasionally, as I'm counseling couples, this language difference will surface. The intuitive spouse will describe how the other makes them feel. The meticulous spouse will ask for a specific example. And the intuitive spouse won't be able to think of one.

They can't. In my example, the intuitive person didn't notice the dust on the mantle, the stain on the carpet, or the poor lighting. They simply understood the overall feeling they experienced. They can easily describe the big picture. But if asked why they thought the room was dingy, they might say, "I don't know. I guess it was a little dark. It just felt dingy, you know?" The intuitive person is often blind to details unless they're consciously looking for them.

Nevertheless, the intuitive person is still correct in their observation. They just might struggle to identify specific details.

This can be a challenge for the meticulous person during a marriage conflict with an intuitive person. The meticulous spouse probably doesn't realize or understand how their specific behaviors are contributing to their spouse's big-picture concerns, and the intuitive spouse probably has a hard time defining why they feel the way they do.

Often, the intuitive spouse offers a generic response like, "Whenever we're with my family, you make me feel this way."

To this, the meticulous spouse might reply, "What? Last time we were with your family, I did this, this, and this. I don't see how any of that could have possibly made you feel that way."

The intuitive spouse feels invalidated and the meticulous spouse feels vindicated, but the same problem exists.

If you have this same communication barrier in your marriage, it can be helpful for the meticulous spouse to say something like, "I never want to make you feel that way. Will you please point out to me in the moment whenever I'm doing what you're describing? I want to work on it for your sake, but I need help seeing the specific behaviors that are hurting you."

Relational vs. Task-Oriented

When I drive, I like to conquer the journey. I like to plan and execute the most efficient route, even if it only saves about thirty seconds of drive time. I often forget to talk to the people in the car. I'm focused on my winning strategy and can't afford distractions.

Robin, on the other hand, cherishes the journey. For her, driving is about enjoyment. She takes back roads to and from work, even though there's a perfectly good expressway between there and our home. People in the car are there to play games, tell stories, make jokes, chat with, and pass the time. They're a welcome distraction from the drive.

One could perhaps blame this difference on introversion versus extroversion, but I think it may go deeper than that. At its core is a prioritization of tasks or people.

The Lord has confronted me about this many times. Just as I described regarding logic and emotion, I can often jump immediately into problem-solving mode when Robin simply wants connection. It's a constant growth area for me.

This has been a difficult chapter for me to write—not because I don't know what I'm talking about but because Robin is home today and is far more interested in spending time with me than letting me write. Five times, I've closed my laptop and spent time with her until she walked away, and I could return to my work. But I've learned that my wife matters more than whatever task I have in front of me, so I've taken some extra-long breaks to eat breakfast together and chat.

Having said that, at times, a task must be finished specifically because your spouse matters. Someone must earn money to care for the family. Someone must clean the house so it doesn't fall apart. Someone must pay the bills so you can have electricity, water, and so on. Task orientation can be healthy, as long as it's a means of conveying love.

But when your project isn't on a tight deadline, it's probably best to step away from your work for a bit and show your love.

(Here she comes again. I'll be back in a moment.)

Cultivating Honor

Language is part of culture. What was the culture of your home growing up? What is the culture of your primary friend groups? Any culture that doesn't look like heaven needs to be left in the dust.

When I was a teenager, my friend group's pecking order was determined by the wittiest sarcasm. I learned to blurt out whatever snarky thought popped into my head, and I quickly rose through the ranks. I had clever (and not-so-clever) nicknames for my friends that highlighted something awkward or funny about them. Everyone thought I was hilarious, except whoever was on the receiving end of my most recent joke.

When Robin and I started dating, she became the focus of my attention, which meant she was most often the target of my well-intentioned bullying. It didn't go well, and I needed correction.

A couple of years into our dating relationship, I helped a pastor and mentor of mine start a new church. Pastor Dan, who had experienced the sharp end of my wit, said, "The sarcasm has to stop. Did you know that the root of the word sarcasm is *sarx,* which is the Greek word for flesh? The original meaning of the word was to tear flesh like a dog. When you employ sarcasm—no matter how well-meaning you are—you're just ripping someone else's flesh. It brings death, not life."

I soon discovered that my sarcasm stemmed from my own insecurities. I thought it made me popular or powerful. Perhaps that was true in a group of immature teenagers, but I no longer have relationships with any of those people. I do have relationship with Robin and Pastor Dan. Apparently, my sarcasm never built anything of lasting value. In my insecurity, I had jockeyed for position in a group that ended up not meaning much. Meanwhile, I rehearsed a skill that damaged those who mattered most.

Contrary to the culture I had embraced, Scripture commands us to honor others above ourselves (Romans 12:10). This includes honoring people in how we listen and speak.

Listening with Honor

All unhealthy communication—sarcasm, mocking, emotional manipulation, the silent treatment, meltdowns, tantrums, etc.—is the fruit of insecurity. When people express any of these tactics, I no longer receive or internalize their words. I recognize them as red flags indicating the other person's present feelings of insecurity, and I look for ways to make them feel secure. When playfulness is not apparent or enjoyed, I call them out or correct them in love, letting them know that I care about them and don't want to participate in the dysfunction.

Offer your spouse the benefit of the doubt. They probably would have never said what they did if they weren't feeling insecure. Those words aren't true indicators of who you are; they're indicators of your spouse's current feelings of insecurity. Your decision to respond in love may be the mechanism God uses to help your spouse feel secure and loved.

If my wife is getting worked up emotionally, it has nothing to do with my identity (though it may have to do with my behavior). If my behavior doesn't warrant her response, then her response probably indicates the presence of a wound. I can be sensitive to that and help her heal and grow in the Lord.

I have to see that I'm not under attack, no matter who is speaking. Even though someone's anger or vitriol might be purposely directed at me, I'm no more under attack than a stone castle is when a group of toddlers throws rocks at it. I don't have to feel like it undermines my identity or integrity. How people perceive me changes nothing about how my Father sees me.

By listening with compassion in this way, I find myself not assuming the worst possible meanings or motives in others. Many times, this has spared me from taking offense and helped me connect with the person's intended meaning. This skill is useful in all of life, but especially in marriage.

Speaking with Honor

Secure communication comes from secure emotions. Jesus said, "A good man brings good things out of the good stored up in his heart, and an evil man brings evil things out of the evil stored up in his heart. For the mouth speaks what the heart is full of" (Luke 6:45).

What are you storing up in your heart? Your spouse's heart might be overflowing with insecurity. What is the overflow of your heart? Are you filling your heart with thoughts that align with God's voice? You can tell what you're storing up in your heart by what is coming out of your mouth.

As Paul instructed in Philippians 4:8, "Finally, brothers and sisters, whatever is true, whatever is noble, whatever is right, whatever is pure, whatever is lovely, whatever is admirable—if anything is excellent or praiseworthy—think about such things."

If you obey this biblical command, you'll find you don't have time to think about the way your spouse mistreated you, how unfair their accusations are, how hypocritical they are, or anything else of the sort. Instead, you'll store up pure, lovely, admirable, excellent, and praiseworthy truths in your heart, and they'll overflow in your words and actions.

If your speech dishonors others, a great solution is to look at what you're holding in your heart. What wounds and sinful judgments are lurking under the surface, affecting not only your perceptions but also how you express yourself? Your spouse is not the parent or sibling who hurt you. Until you address the lies you're meditating on, you'll probably have a terrible time trying to change your behavior.

I have often told my church that traumas try to teach us lies. If believed, those lies become lenses through which we view the world, others, the Lord, and ourselves. They distort reality and lead to future misunderstandings and sinful assumptions. Naturally, if we're not anchored in truth but are believing a distorted reality, the overflow of our hearts will reflect that distorted reality rather than the peace of God's kingdom.

When we surrender our sinful judgments to the cross and receive God's truth in their place, we suddenly find our behaviors and attitudes changing as well. The overflow of our heart changes, which is naturally reflected in our speech.

Good News for Your Marriage ~ Art Thomas

Most of us don't have communication problems; we have heart problems, which are really gospel problems. Yes, cultural differences might make us lean toward direct or indirect speech, logic or emotion, meticulous perception or intuitive, and so on. But all these are easily overcome by a couple who purposes to love each other.

How we interpret each other is directly related to how we view each other. Our expectations color our perceptions. Sinful judgments cloud our discernment and make us fall victim to offense when none was intended. But when we give each other the benefit of the doubt, trusting in the other's love for us, we can look past any unclear or confusing language and see a heart that wants connection with us. Choose love.

Gathering Your Thoughts

Write down your thoughts about these questions before talking to your spouse about this chapter. Talk to the Lord about any shortcomings you see in yourself, and simply trust him to immediately bring forgiveness, freedom, and transformation to your heart.

1. Do you tend to communicate more directly or indirectly? How about your spouse? Do you feel like the two of you connect well in this regard?
2. Do you tend to prioritize logic or emotion? How about your spouse? Do you feel like the two of you connect well in this regard?
3. Do you find that your perception of the world is more perceptive or intuitive? How about your spouse? Do you feel like the two of you connect well in this regard?
4. Do you tend to be more relational or task-oriented? How about your spouse? Do you feel like the two of you connect well in this regard?
5. What are some pure, lovely, admirable, excellent, and praiseworthy truths about your spouse and their love for you that you can remind yourself of? Write them down.

Conversation Starters

Open up to your spouse about the following topics. Require nothing from them—only give.

1. Share what impacted you most about this chapter.
2. If you have recognized any dishonoring language that you have expressed toward your spouse, identify it and apologize.
3. Share with your spouse the virtuous thoughts you wrote about them in #5 of the previous activity.
4. If you feel like you've noticed some communication barriers in your relationship, tell your spouse what you learned. Be sure to do so in a nonaccusatory way that invites your spouse closer without making them feel demeaned or unappreciated.

Ask your spouse the following:

1. Are there any ways we interact that make you feel dishonored or undervalued?
2. Is there anything I can do to help you feel valued and heard?

CHAPTER 12:

The Pathway to Intimacy

AFTER THE PEOPLE OF ISRAEL LEFT EGYPT AND CROSSED THE Red Sea, they came to Mount Sinai. There God gave them the law. A significant portion of God's instructions were devoted to how the people were to worship him and maintain right relationship with him.

As Moses met with God on the mountain, God showed him the design of his heavenly abode (Hebrews 8:5). God gave Moses specific instructions for building a mobile replica of that spiritual reality—a tabernacle or tent where God would dwell with his people as they journeyed to the promised land.

God wasn't only specific with the details of the tabernacle's design, but he also gave comprehensive instructions about how his people were to approach him in the tabernacle. God chose Israel out of all the nations to be intimate with him, and then he told them the exact protocol for that intimacy to benefit them. In many cases, to breech that protocol could mean death, so God made sure they knew the right way to approach.

While many books have been written about the tabernacle and while many different analogies can be drawn, I want to explore a little of what the tabernacle can teach us about human intimacy. Since we are made in God's image and likeness, we can reasonably conclude that the right way to approach intimacy with God can give insight into the right way to approach intimacy with each other. And when we breech that protocol, what we're left with is sin and death—falling short of the glory.

When many people hear the word *intimacy*, they automatically think about sex. But there is a lot to explore in the realm of intimacy before reaching the most intimate place of sexual union.

Glorious sex begins at the outer gate and moves to the inner sanctuary. When sex is undesired or unenjoyable, it's often because one or more of the steps along the way to that most intimate place have been neglected or violated (this is not to overlook physical conditions that may require medical intervention or advice). But God has shown us how to rightly approach such holy fellowship. If you understand how to approach intimacy with God, you will understand how to approach intimacy with your spouse.

Entering Sacred Space

Those who entered through the outer gate of the tabernacle did so for purposes of worship. The outer court wasn't a nice field to casually walk through. It wasn't a space for conducting business. It was a place of blood, guts, fire, and smoke—animal sacrifices and priestly rituals. It was a place entered only to seek the Lord.

This is part of why Jesus fashioned a whip and drove the money changers and businesspeople out of the temple courts, flipping their tables, scattering their coins, and dispersing the animals they sought to sell (John 2:13–17). Those people entered the space meant for relating to God and instead

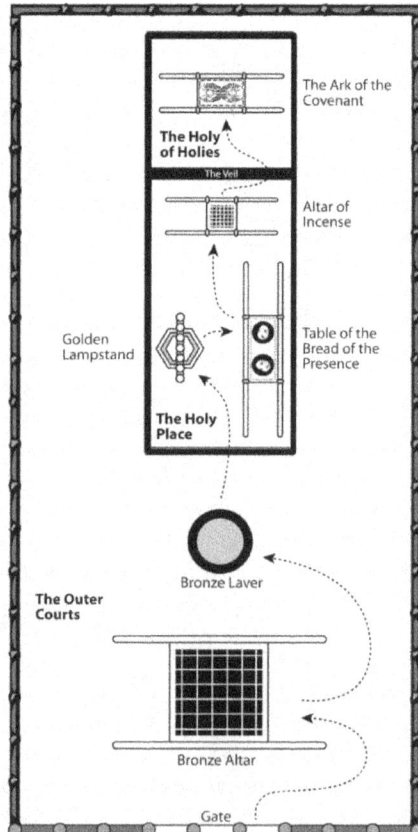

The Ark of the Covenant

The Holy of Holies

The Veil

Altar of Incense

Golden Lampstand

Table of the Bread of the Presence

The Holy Place

Bronze Laver

The Outer Courts

Bronze Altar

Gate

used it for their own benefit. There is no room for self-serving motives in the presence of God.

Psalm 100:4 instructs us to "enter his gates with thanksgiving and his courts with praise; give thanks to him and praise his name." The right way to approach relationship with God is for his sake and not our own. Certainly, we will benefit more than he will, but we come declaring his value and worth, grateful in our hearts to be in his presence. When we come only for our sake and not reverently for his sake, we're like the money changers Jesus chased out with a whip.

Similarly, when we enter any sort of relational space with others, there is no room for self-serving motives. Even if we will ultimately benefit more than the other person, the posture of our hearts should be gratitude and honor for the other, treating relationship with that person as sacred space. We surrender every ounce of extortion and manipulation and come to love and serve.

No one deserves to be in the relational space of another. No one can earn their way into relationship with anyone. There is no room for entitlement in relationship. We are welcomed into this realm by the one who lives there. Those who selflessly enter relationship for the sake of the other are most likely to be welcomed into that space.

The Altar of Surrender

The first fixture of the tabernacle upon entering was a large bronze altar (Exodus 40:6). Every day, a variety of sacrifices were offered on this altar (Leviticus 1–7). The fire on the altar was to be kept burning at all times, always ready to receive a sacrifice (Leviticus 6:12–13). Whether animals or grain, various offerings were made on the altar—some to cover sin, some as expressions of worship, others to make the worshipper ritually clean so he could approach God, and still others as expressions of gratitude that relationship had been restored, and so on.

At the altar, sin was confronted, acknowledged, and finished. It was a place of sacrifice, forgiveness, and reconciliation. It was a place of valuing God above self.

Once we've entered into relationship with someone, the pathway of intimacy begins with these same principles. Consider how Paul's instructions to believers demonstrate the altar:

Love must be sincere. Hate what is evil; cling to what is good. Be devoted to one another in love. Honor one another above yourselves. Never be lacking in zeal, but keep your spiritual fervor, serving the Lord. Be joyful in hope, patient in affliction, faithful in prayer. Share with the Lord's people who are in need. Practice hospitality.

Bless those who persecute you; bless and do not curse. Rejoice with those who rejoice; mourn with those who mourn. Live in harmony with one another. Do not be proud, but be willing to associate with people of low position. Do not be conceited.

Do not repay anyone evil for evil. Be careful to do what is right in the eyes of everyone. If it is possible, as far as it depends on you, live at peace with everyone. Do not take revenge, my dear friends, but leave room for God's wrath, for it is written: "It is mine to avenge; I will repay," says the Lord. (Romans 9:9–19)

Intimacy begins with devotion to the other in love, honoring them above oneself. Like the fire that was always kept burning, we keep our spiritual fervor, serving the Lord—revering him through submission to others (Ephesians 5:21). We serve others with generosity and hospitality, caring for their needs. We don't take revenge. Instead, we are quick to forgive and willingly self-sacrifice for the sake of peace.

In short, the altar is where relationship is made right. It's the first order of business as we get to know each other. The altar is still a long way from the most intimate place in the tabernacle, so those who approach sex before addressing sin and selfishness are sure to have problems. Intimacy requires right standing with one another, and only the blood of Jesus can accomplish that.

If you've sinned against your spouse—even if they're unaware of it—start by making your relationship right. Until that's settled, sex should be the last thing you're pursuing. Ask forgiveness and give your spouse room to process their feelings.

Likewise, if your spouse has sinned against you, confront them about it. This isn't about withholding sex from them as much as it is about inviting sex in the proper way. We don't confront sin to push the other person away but to draw them closer.

And certainly, when your relationship is right before each other and God, the altar becomes a place of gratitude. Celebrate your healthy relationship. Talk about what you like in your friendship with each other. Take a moment now and then to consciously rejoice in your love for the other person and how much they mean to you. Don't be afraid to verbally express those feelings to them.

The Washing of the Word

After the priests offered sacrifices at the altar, they couldn't enter the Tent of Meeting until they first cleansed themselves at a bronze washbasin (called a laver).

We learn in the New Testament that Jesus washes us with "the washing with water through the word" (Ephesians 5:26). God's voice cleanses us and removes everything that doesn't belong. When talking about God as a gardener pruning a vine to make it more fruitful, Jesus told his disciples, "You are already clean because of the word I have spoken to you" (John 15:3).

As God's words wash over us, they either expose unaddressed impurities that need to be surrendered to the altar or invite us to approach his presence. Either way, it's an invitation into closer relationship. In our relationship with the Lord, we are first made right with him through the blood of Jesus, offered on the altar of the cross. But then he beckons us closer. No one comes to Jesus unless they hear the Father's voice drawing them into that relationship (John 6:44–45).

At the laver, God gave the priests a means to ceremonially cleanse themselves so that they could rightly enter the Tent of Meeting and minister to him. Likewise, in our human relationships, we have to be invited into someone's inner world.

Certainly, on your wedding day, you permanently opened your inner world to your spouse. By choosing to be married, you were saying, "I want you in the deep places of my heart. You are welcome here." So in many ways, there is a standing invitation for the married couple.

But at the same time, the priests had to cleanse their feet and hands every time they were about to enter the tent—especially if they had been offering bloody sacrifices on the altar.

If a sinful breech of relationship needed to be addressed at the altar, it's best to let the other person invite you back into that place of deeper intimacy. You cannot force your way in before they're ready and expect your interactions to go well.

Honor the other person by letting them set the terms of how ready they are for deeper intimacy.

Tending to the Lampstand

The tabernacle consisted of three basic parts. Outside the Tent of Meeting was the outer court, containing the bronze altar and laver, surrounded by a curtain. In this outside area, even those who weren't priests were welcomed to pray and worship. We can have many relationships that are no more intimate than the outer court. We love these people and have a certain amount of access to each other, but our relationships don't go very deep.

But in the Tent of Meeting only those permitted can enter. Inside the Tent of Meeting were two rooms; the first was called the Holy Place. In this room, the priests performed their duties, day and night. It was intimate in that it was hidden from the rest of the people in the outer courts. But it was not exclusive. Many priests traversed this space. If the outer court is a space of casual friendship, the Holy Place is a space of close friendship.

In the Holy Place stood a golden lampstand. This special seven-branched lamp was filled with oil, which often represents the Holy Spirit in Scripture. The lampstand was to be tended all night long so that the flames would never go out (Leviticus 24:1–4).

In our relationship with God, we are invited into lifestyles of vigilance, keeping our lamps burning and full of oil. When Jesus used this language in the parable of the ten virgins in Matthew 25:1–13, he also told two other parables about being faithful with what God entrusts to us and serving others. He said, "Whatever you did for one of the least of these brothers and sisters of mine, you did for me" (Matthew 25:40). Vigilance in our relationship with God is a matter of being attentive to Jesus's needs, filled with oil— empowered by the Holy Spirit.

Likewise, in our human relationships, the place of close friendship is a place of attentiveness to each other's needs. We take note of each other's emotional condition. We watch for physical needs. When even one of the seven flames begins to flicker, we add more oil. We care for our friend and serve them.

The degree of attentiveness will vary from person to person. But the closer the relationship, the more responsible you are to watch the other's flame and help keep them burning. Certainly, marriage is the most intimate covenant with another, and therefore, you bear the most responsibility for your spouse to cherish them with your attention. Like the priest sacrificing his own sleep to tend the lampstand all night, prioritize your spouse's needs above your own. It's part of intimacy.

The Table of Presence

Also in the Holy Place was a golden table with a blue tablecloth and plates. There, twelve loaves of special bread were set out every Sabbath on behalf of the twelve tribes of Israel, made from the finest flour. This bread of the presence was an offering to the Lord, but the priests were to eat it there in the Holy Place (Leviticus 24:1–9).

The Bible uses bread in a variety of metaphors, sometimes representing an army, a nation, an answered prayer, physical provision, or even Jesus himself. But in this direct context, we see a special, sacred place of fellowship—a table in the Tent of Meeting where priests ate God's bread in his presence.

When the New Testament church came along, God's people "broke bread in their homes and ate together with glad and sincere hearts" (Acts 2:46). When we gather at the same table and eat together, we engage in friendship differently than when we merely participate in shared activities. We are face to face. There is a give-and-take of conversation—if not, then the always talking party will go hungry as they never take time to chew and listen to the other.

The table of the bread of the presence is an invitation to deep fellowship and brotherly love with God. It's a place of vulnerability and affection. It's a place of laughter and fun. In short, it's a place of intimate friendship. Some want to enjoy this space without first going to the altar with sin or hearing God's invitation or being attentive to his needs. But this table is reached through right relationship and reverence. The pathway matters.

In human relationships, some people are easy to welcome into this space. The two of you simply get along and enjoy each other's presence without effort. Some may marry such a person, but others struggle to feel such ease. Friendship with your spouse must be cultivated. And because your spouse is your most important relationship, friendship with him or her must be prioritized above all other friendships.

If you don't feel like you and your spouse are friends like you want to be, start at the gate of the outer court, and follow the pathway laid out for entering the deeper places of God's temple. Then, have fun together. Go on dates. Goof off and crack jokes. And most importantly, be present with the other. Look them in the eye. Smile at them. Hold their hand. Share a meal and a deep conversation about life and your future together. Dream out loud together. Make time to enjoy each other's company.

Incense and Listening

The last item in the Holy Place, before entering the innermost room, was a golden altar of incense. Through the apostle John's prophecy, we learn that this incense represents the prayers of God's people (Revelation 5:8; 8:3–4). In Psalm 141:2, David sang, "May my prayer be set before you like incense."

When someone starts burning incense, it's impossible for anyone in the room to ignore. Your willingness to make your needs and desires known to God is a pleasing aroma to him. He loves to hear you bring your requests because it means you trust him.

Having said that, God gave specific instructions about the ingredients that composed this incense. No other incense was to be used on the altar (Exodus 30:34–37). Whatever requests we make of the Lord must come from a place of honoring him. As 1 John 5:14 says, "This is the confidence we have in approaching God: that if we ask anything *according to his will*, he hears us" (emphasis added).

Intimate friends want to love each other. I never feel burdened when a close friend makes a request of me. Close friends honor each other with their requests and don't take advantage of each other. They ask respectfully, trusting in the other's love and character.

Also, God commanded that this incense was not to be used anywhere other than the Holy Place (Exodus 30:38). The requests made at this level of friendship are special. They're intimate.

They're not surface-level requests that one might make of someone in the outer courts, like, "Can you pick me up from the airport?" Instead, someone might ask a close friend to be responsible for their children should something happen to them. Or a woman might ask a close friend to be with her as she delivers a baby. Or a man might ask a close friend to join him in an outing that he usually enjoys alone, like hunting or fishing.

Beyond this, certain requests made inside marriage belong in no other relationship. Conversations about what we want to try in the marriage bed are healthy when they are free of selfishness and full of trust. Our love and respect for the other person offers oneself and does not demand from the other. Certainly, we can be vulnerable about what we like, but this, too, should come from a place of offering your spouse a look into your heart, not a place of manipulation and mere thrill-seeking. Have those intimate conversations with your spouse. When the protocol for intimacy has been followed and all the other needs are met, conversations like these are more likely to be welcomed and enjoyed.

The Holy of Holies

A thick curtain stood between the Holy Place and the Most Holy Place, also known as the holy of holies. This innermost room of the tabernacle held the ark of the covenant—a golden box containing hidden reminders of God's covenant with his people. And there, above that ark, God manifested himself.

This room was not for just anyone. It wasn't even available to the priests who served in the Holy Place. This room was only for the one high priest and could only be entered when all the other protocols and requirements had been met (Hebrews 9:6–7). Still today, in God's real heavenly house, only the High Priest, Jesus, is allowed to enter this place of deepest communion with the Father. Thankfully, because we are cleansed by Jesus's blood and living in union with him as his body, we, too, can "approach God's throne of grace with confidence" (Hebrews 4:16). Jesus has entered this innermost place of intimacy "on our behalf" (Hebrews 6:20). Because he is there, we are there.

In our relationship with God, in the throne room—the holy of holies—our friendship with God is elevated to a covenantal union like none other. It's where we "receive mercy and find grace to help us in our time of need" (Hebrews 4:16). It's a place of spiritual ecstasy and rejoicing in one another. And this inner chamber of union with God is represented by the inner chamber of union between husband and wife.

> Let him kiss me with the kisses of his mouth—
> for your love is more delightful than wine.
> Pleasing is the fragrance of your perfumes;
> your name is like perfume poured out.
> No wonder the young women love you!
> Take me away with you—let us hurry!
> Let the king bring me into his chambers.
> (Song of Songs 1:2–4)

You can have many casual friends in the outer court. You can have a handful of close friends in the Holy Place. But only one's spouse is authorized to press past the veil and enter this space of complete vulnerability, covenant, deep intimacy, and union.

Remember, marriage is designed by God to be a prophetic picture of Christ and the church. You don't generally start at the place of revealing this union perfectly, but you can be conformed more and more into this image through humble intentionality and trust in God's grace. You may not be at this place yet with your spouse, but if you will commit yourselves to the entire pathway to intimacy, you will encounter a place of marital union where you and your spouse trust each other and know each other enough to say, "Come boldly to this most sacred space."

Gathering Your Thoughts

Write down your thoughts about these questions before talking to your spouse about this chapter. Talk to the Lord about any shortcomings you see in yourself, and simply trust him to immediately bring forgiveness, freedom, and transformation to your heart.

1. Consider the pathway to intimacy that God laid out: enter his gates with gratitude, deal with sin at the altar, value his words that wash and cleanse you, be attentive to his desires through worship and obedience, fellowship with him as a friend, pray big prayers, and enjoy union with him. Jesus does all the work to bring us to God. He is the Way, the sacrificial Lamb, the Word, the Light of the World, the Bread of Life, and our constant Intercessor. But if we're not relying on him in these various ways, we can find ourselves struggling to engage in intimacy with God. Let the Holy Spirit examine your faith and relationship with God. Do you need to surrender any sin to him? Have you taken God's voice for granted? Are you self-centered rather than living for the Lord? Have you let your friendship and enjoyment of the Lord grow cold? How is your prayer life? God welcomes you into the Most Holy Place, and he sent his Son to make a way for you. Take a moment to pray about each stage along the pathway, and let the Lord bring repentance to your heart as needed. Journal your realizations and experiences.

2. Now, consider the same pathway concerning your relationship with your spouse. Are you choosing relationship with them in gratitude and joy? Do you need to address any sin issues between you? Do you need to invite your spouse into a place of closer intimacy? Are you being attentive to their needs? Do you feel that your friendship is healthy? Do you demonstrate deep-level trust in your spouse? Is your sexual intimacy thriving? If you recognize a breech in the pathway to intimacy, ask the Lord how to restore health to that aspect of your relationship, and journal what thoughts come to mind.

Conversation Starters

Open up to your spouse about the following topics. Require nothing from them—only give.

1. Share what impacted you most about this chapter.
2. Be vulnerable with your spouse about your relationship with God. Talk about any areas where you feel God helped you see a need for growth. Ask your spouse if they have any ideas that might help you grow in your relationship with God.
3. Apologize for any ways you might recognize that you have been inattentive or careless with regard to one or more of the stages toward intimacy.
4. If you need to address a present sin issue in your relationship, confess your own sin first, and then humbly ask the other if they're okay with bringing up any concerns you see in their life. If they're not, ask them when they think they'll be ready.

Ask your spouse the following:

1. Are there any aspects of our lives in which you don't feel as close to me as you want to be?

CHAPTER 13:

For Your Eyes Only

GOD DESIGNED US FOR INTIMACY WITH HIM, AND THEN HE made us in his image and likeness. Romans 1:20 tells us that "since the creation of the world God's invisible qualities—his eternal power and divine nature—have been clearly seen, being understood from what has been made." Everything God created reveals an aspect of his nature.

Who designed the human body? Who invented sexuality? Whose idea was the orgasm?

These creations are not dirty or a distraction from greater matters. They are good and holy. They exist to reveal God's nature to us. The powers of darkness seek to pervert them so that what they reveal about God is twisted and broken. That's the nature of sin—falling short of the glory.

Remember, sin is the broken image of God. Sexual sin is a distorted picture of our relationship with God. Sexual sin says, "You exist for my pleasure," rather than "I have chosen you and desire to bring you joy and fulfillment." Sexual sin elevates the desires of the flesh over the beauty of God's design. Like Esau selling his birthright for a bowl of stew, it prioritizes momentary gratification over eternal bliss (Genesis 25:29–34).

God's rules about sex only happening between one biological man and one biological woman inside the covenant of marriage are not meant as a means of merely policing human behavior to control us. They are to protect us physically, emotionally, psychologically, socially, and spiritually. And they preserve the integrity of an activity that prophetically invites humanity into a beautiful union with God that is far greater than marital sex—a union that has eternal ramifications.

If *right* sex is a prophetic picture of Christ and the church, then *wrong* sex also prophesies but does so falsely.

Like any false prophet, this distortion of God's voice leads people astray. Wrong sex teaches people to live for their own pleasure. It lowers glorious union to the level of mere animal instinct, mocking self-control and covenant commitment.

Today's culture platforms this false prophet. Comedies, dramas, action, and even documentaries, the news, commercials, and so-called reality-shows all present this false prophet to the masses.

I believe the church ought to speak candidly about holy sex. If the church isn't discussing sex, then from where will people receive their information? I want to prepare you that in this chapter, while I will not be crass, some of what I say will be graphic. I will be appropriate but clear. If you find yourself triggered negatively by what you read, use the tools you learned in chapter 8 to seek transformation and healing from the Lord. You may even find that this chapter brings tremendous healing as the distortions of sin are cleared away and God's nature is made apparent.

I understand that sexuality can be an uncomfortable topic for a lot of people. Many have been deeply damaged by sexual abuse, shame, unhealthy role models, poor education, and violations of boundaries, causing sex to be undesirable and perhaps even unpleasant. My goal in this chapter is not to ignore these tragedies and emotional pains but to present sex as God intended, hopefully bringing healing to those who need a righteous revelation of sexuality. My goal is to platform the true prophecies of right sex.

Sex is designed by God to be enjoyable. If it's not enjoyable, it's important to find out why. Is there a physical issue, like pain or discomfort? Talk to your medical doctor. Is there an emotional or psychological issue? You may need the Lord to help you work through painful past experiences—forgiving people, discovering truth, and renouncing lies learned from trauma and disappointment. Is there a relational issue? Consider the steps along the pathway to intimacy discussed in the previous chapter to make sure all the important areas are being fulfilled. In all these areas, a licensed Christian counselor who specializes in matters of sexuality may be a tremendous help.

Sex as God designed it is a beautiful, holy act that reveals some of God's invisible qualities. It is an opportunity to physically communicate the gospel to your spouse. The bride and Bridegroom become one as Christ first self-sacrifices for the sake of the church, the church then opens herself up to his love and presence, and he enters her, depositing the life-giving seed of his Spirit and grace in a mutually experienced celebration of love, intimacy, and ecstasy.

Selfless Sex

God didn't create us with selfishness hardwired into our bodies. Sin reoriented the human sex drive toward selfishness. That means a redeemed Christian sex drive is best expressed in selflessness.

Experts on the subject have noted that the female anatomy is such that only a minority of women experience orgasm through regular intercourse.[38] Generally speaking, the female orgasm requires attention to both emotions and physiology. Women typically need to feel secure, loved, desirable, and aroused for sex to be enjoyable; and then, generally speaking, clitoral stimulation is often needed to reach climax. It would seem, then, that God designed sex to be most enjoyable when the husband is genuinely selfless, like Jesus.[39]

Similarly, the wife selflessly opens herself to her husband, welcoming him into her own body. In this reception, the husband experiences emotional pleasure that cannot be gained from a reluctant partner.

God designed men and women in such a way that our greatest sense of biological ecstasy comes from mutually exercising selfless affection in the security and integrity of marital covenant.

---

[38] Sheila Wray Gregoire, Rebecca Gregoire Lindenbach, Joanna Sawatsky, *The Great Sex Rescue*, (Grand Rapids, Michigan: Baker Books, 2021), Kindle Edition, 2021, 47.

[39] Sheila Wray Gregoire, *31 Days to Great Sex*, (Grand Rapids, Michigan: Zondervan, 2020), 135–36.

Outside the covenant of marriage, selflessness looks like worshipping God with one's body—loving him with chastity and zeal for his return, despite the struggle and sacrifice. But inside marriage, this selflessness looks like serving one's spouse as a prophetic picture of Christ and the church.

The challenge, however, is that many preachers and teachers have framed selfless sex as catering to someone else's selfishness. If a spouse (usually the husband) wants sex, they argue, then the other spouse (usually the wife) has to give it to them, even if the second spouse hates it. They base their teaching on the following passage:

> The husband should fulfill his marital duty to his wife, and likewise the wife to her husband. The wife does not have authority over her own body but yields it to her husband. In the same way, the husband does not have authority over his own body but yields it to his wife. Do not deprive each other except perhaps by mutual consent and for a time, so that you may devote yourselves to prayer. Then come together again so that Satan will not tempt you because of your lack of self-control. (1 Corinthians 7:3–5)

I would argue that the popular interpretation of this passage promotes selfishness. It can lead to spouses using each other as sexual objects for their own gratification whenever desired. The other spouse is simply expected to smile and participate whether or not they like it. But this would be inconsistent with everything else the Bible teaches about love.

As 1 Corinthians 13:5 tells us, love "is not self-seeking," so I would suggest that a better interpretation of this passage exists.

Notice that when Paul speaks of yielding authority over one's body to their spouse, he follows it with a command not to deprive each other. Deprive each other of what? Arguably, the answer is an orgasm.

This means Paul expects a husband and a wife to view each other as their only source of orgasm. If a husband doesn't give his wife an orgasm, she will be deprived of it because she's not going to seek it apart from him, and vice versa.

A better interpretation of this passage is that husbands and wives have yielded authority over their own orgasms, trusting the other not to deprive them but to fulfill their marital duty in selfless love. Scripture invites you to give your spouse regular orgasms, not use your spouse to achieve your own.

In this view, when a man and woman marry, the husband no longer has authority over his own orgasm but surrenders that authority to his wife as a gift she can give him. Likewise, the wife no longer has authority over her own orgasm but surrenders that authority to her husband as a gift he can give her. Accordingly, sex becomes less about acquiring pleasure and more about giving pleasure.

When you're "in the mood," don't think of yourself as needing something *from* your spouse but rather as having something *for* your spouse. Your sex drive is a gift to give to your spouse, not an appetite to satiate by using your spouse. Focus your attention on wooing them and building their excitement for how you want to serve them. Let your sex drive encourage you to be creative and fun in your foreplay as you aim to make the upcoming intercourse the most enjoyable experience for your spouse that you can.

When you're not in the mood for sex, the principle of selflessness still applies. Certainly, at times, perhaps due to sickness, injury, or exhaustion, sex just isn't in the cards. But many times, a less interested partner can be wooed. Just tell your spouse that you need a little more foreplay before you're ready. "Yes, but help me" is not "no." It's a willingness to be aroused even when sex is not yet on your mind.

But remember the pathway to intimacy. If you're not in the mood because of a relational issue that needs to be resolved, address that first. No amount of foreplay will eliminate the need for reconciliation, friendship, and connection in your relationship. You're not obligated to ignore festering relational problems for the sake of a biological release.

Nevertheless, there's a fine line between saying, "Can we wait on that until we deal with this issue?" and saying, "I'm not having sex with you until you behave the way I want." The latter is manipulation, not selflessness. "Wait" means "I love you, but I want all of you, not just your genitals, so let's work through our emotional and relational issues on the pathway to sex." But silently withholding sex as punishment comes from a place of unforgiveness and a lack of desire for real reconciliation or intimacy. Be careful that if you're delaying sex, it's for selfless reasons and not selfish ones.

Furthermore, many couples struggle because one partner has a chronically low sex drive, health issues that hinder sexual activity, long-term exhaustion from work or parenting, clinical depression, or general disinterest in sex. If your spouse experiences any of these issues, you may deal with feelings of rejection, wondering why your spouse won't receive your advances.

But remember that you're not in this for yourself. Turn to the Lord for emotional fulfillment and aim to selflessly love your spouse in nonsexual ways. Devote yourself to being intimate with them in all the ways described in the previous chapter, strengthening your entire pathway to intimacy. Aim to understand your spouse's struggle, and love them through it. When appropriate, be flirtatious with no strings attached—have fun with your spouse without any pressure to engage in sex. Perhaps an interest in sex will grow in your partner, but even if it doesn't, you'll feel closer and more fulfilled than if you focus on yourself.

Pure and Spotless Lovers

As stewards of each other's orgasms, you have a responsibility to your spouse, and that responsibility begins in the heart before it ever becomes a sexual act.

Jesus will one day return for a pure and spotless bride (2 Corinthians 11:2; Ephesians 5:27; Revelation 19:7). This doesn't mean that only the wife has any sort of responsibility to be transformed. Our Bridegroom is also a pure and spotless sacrifice who lays down his life for us (1 Peter 1:19). The church is being conformed into his likeness, after all.

Eternity will look like a pure and spotless bride being united with her pure and spotless Bridegroom. Accordingly, if we are to be a prophetic revelation of this reality, both husband and wife are to be conformed into the image of the pure and spotless Son of God.

Well-meaning Christians in the last century or so have wisely warned young people against premarital sex, but the way this has often been done can be damaging. When we use language like "keep yourself pure for marriage," we imply that sex outside of marriage makes someone irreparably impure. Thus, many Christians today view themselves (and others) as "damaged goods"—tainted by sin and regretfully unable to offer their spouse the full value of themselves.

But purity is not produced from the outside. Jesus railed against the Pharisees for focusing on external regulations while ignoring purity of heart (Matthew 23:25–28). One can avoid sex until marriage and yet still not be a pure and spotless spouse. As Jesus explained, "First clean the inside of the cup and dish, and then the outside also will be clean" (Matthew 23:26).

Praise God for those who kept themselves from sex before marriage. Their testimony reveals the grace and power of God to keep us free and self-controlled. But those who engaged in broken, worldly sex need not own it as their identities. Rather, through faith in Christ, they, too, have a testimony of God's grace and power to cleanse sin and bestow purity.

Many married couples engaged in sex prior to their weddings. Some married because of a pregnancy, either wanting or being pressured to take responsibility. Others perhaps messed around before their wedding without a pregnancy, but they married to make it right. Marriage may have established a proper context for their ongoing sexual activity, but marriage vows do not erase past sin. Only the blood of Jesus can do that (Hebrews 9:22). In the words of the old hymn by Robert Lowry,

> *What can wash away my sin?*
> *Nothing but the blood of Jesus.*
> *What can make me whole again?*
> *Nothing but the blood of Jesus.*[40]

Premarital sex—even with one's current spouse—needs to be surrendered to the cross. It must be confessed, rejected as the selfish and foolish act that it was, and thereby removed from the couple's relational identity. Surrender the right to look back on such sin as cute, special, or in any way acceptable. Then, consider

---

[40] Robert Lowry, "Nothing but the Blood," 1876, public domain.

that old way of sin to be dead and move forward as the pure, new creation that you are.

As you allow the Lord to work in your heart, you can enjoy your identity as a pure and spotless spouse. You no longer live; Christ lives in you. Hebrews 10:14 tells us that "by one sacrifice he has made perfect forever those who are being made holy." As long as you're in process, you're perfect. You don't have to live in guilt, shame, and regret of past sins. You can instead enjoy the freedom of Christ's cleansing power.

You can present yourself as pure and spotless to your spouse, even if he or she isn't interested in following Jesus the way you are. You don't have to be afraid that they will defile you with their own impurities. Even if they aren't saved, God sets them apart as holy simply because of your faith (1 Corinthians 7:14).

Remember, godly sex is selfless sex. It invites and gives; it doesn't coerce or demand. You don't need to require your spouse to have a pure heart before giving yourself to them. You simply need to offer your spouse a pure heart. This is how Jesus engages with us before we are fully transformed. We are righteous because he is righteous, even though we're still being transformed into his perfect image. He gives his perfect, pure, and holy self to us long before we can even come close to offering the same.

Attraction and Lust

Before Robin and I were married, I was addicted to pornography. Many have made the mistake of believing that marriage would cure their pornography addiction. It doesn't. The insecurities and emotional struggles that fuel pornography addiction don't magically disappear when you suddenly have a real human to have sex with. Married or not, it's easier to satisfy our selfishness with a cheap thrill than to feign selflessness and do the hard work of intimacy.

Thankfully, the Lord mercifully set me free from that addiction about five years before our wedding. I learned to practice selflessness, valuing intimacy and holiness over a biological release. This has been a tremendous blessing to Robin's and my marriage.

But many marriages have been challenged or even plagued by varying degrees of lust and sexual addiction, including pornography. The faithful spouse feels deep pain and often wonders why their partner didn't consider them to be enough to meet their needs.

Speaking as one who was previously addicted to lust, sinful sensuality, and pornography, I can say with full confidence that freedom is available in Christ. Everything we've discussed so far in this book is part of the solution. My greatest freedom came in confessing my addiction and considering it dead on the cross. With that came forgiving the older boys in my neighborhood who had sexually abused me as a child, forgiving my friend down the street for introducing me to the magazine he found under his dad's bed, forgiving the women who posed for the pictures, forgiving my parents for not protecting me more (as though they could), and even forgiving myself for my own actions and decisions during my seven years of addiction.

Another piece of the puzzle was the struggle within my own conscience. I would notice that a woman was beautiful and quickly feel guilty. And if I noticed enough women were beautiful, I would resign myself to the false belief that I wasn't actually free like I thought, and I'd soon be back in the throes of addiction.

There's a difference between attraction and lust. Attraction is the God-given capacity of human beings to notice, appreciate, and value beauty in all its forms—whether physical, emotional, spiritual, etc. It is both normal and human to notice that someone is attractive. Lust, on the other hand, is the selfish perversion of attraction. It is the desire to have something or someone for one's personal benefit—exploiting beauty (or relishing evil intent) for one's own self-indulgence.

I can notice a woman is attractive and then look away and move on with my day as though nothing happened. That's not sin. Lust is found in the deliberate, self-serving steps that follow. It's what the late Orthodox theologian Paul Evdokimov called "the willed covetous gaze."[41]

Popular Christian culture often treats men as though lust and the objectification of women are hardwired into the male design—meaning these behaviors and mindsets are inevitable and natural aspects of God-given masculinity. But whatever true masculinity

---

[41] Paul Evdokimov, *The Sacrament of Love*, (Yonkers, New York: St. Vladimir's Seminary Press, 1985), 173.

might be, its traits must be found in the image and likeness of God. Anything not found there is only a perversion of our design. And God doesn't have a lust problem.

Meanwhile, women are often counseled as though they are the God-given answer to the male problem of lust—that everything they do or don't do is either helping or hurting men in their struggle. Some Christian professionals have even advised wives to regularly have sex to ensure that their husbands won't want to commit adultery or engage in porn, not realizing that a sinful man will sin regardless of his wife's behavior. A lack of self-control and love is not overcome with more sex.

The truth is that both men and women need to experience the freedom Jesus gives from sinful lust. While women ought not deliberately try to tempt men into sin, women are not responsible for whether men lust. Men and women are each responsible for themselves. No competent adult is a hapless victim of other people's decisions. As Christians, we have the Holy Spirit, and therefore we have self-control (Galatians 5:22–23).

Some have questioned whether lust is appropriate inside marriage. There is never a place for viewing another human as an object. Such selfish use of another is sin because it falls short of the glorious picture of Christ and the church. But God does admire his creation and call it good (Genesis 1:31). Scripture invites a man to "rejoice in the wife of your youth. A loving doe, a graceful deer— may her breasts satisfy you always, may you ever be intoxicated with her love" (Proverbs 5:18–19). Apparently, it is possible to delight in your spouse's body while still valuing him or her as a person to be loved and cherished, not an object to be used.

Sexual arousal is not sin. In James 1, the apostle speaks of temptation and sin in verses 13 through 15, and then in verses 16 and 17, he writes, "Don't be deceived, my dear brothers and sisters. Every good and perfect gift is from above, coming down from the Father of the heavenly lights, who does not change like shifting shadows." Your sex drive is a good, perfect, God-given gift. Arousal, desire, genitals, and everything else God designed about you are all blessings, and he hasn't changed his mind about these revelations of his nature.

Unchecked desire leads to sin, and unchecked sin leads to death (James 1:14–15). But again, sexual arousal is not sin. Yes, with arousal comes a greater challenge to avoid misconduct, but never feel guilty for being aroused. Simply be careful to maintain authority over it with the Holy Spirit's help.

If feelings are escalating in your body and you find that your flesh wants to indulge in sinful activity, shift your attention to Jesus. Begin worshipping him. Pray. Sing. Read. Exercise. Simply move your attention to nonarousing activities until your body calms down. It may even be helpful to confess to your spouse or a Christian friend when temptation feels overwhelming, and ask for prayer.

I found great freedom in recognizing that beauty (and our capacity to recognize it) only exists because God is the archetypal Beauty in the universe. All other beauty is inferior to him and merely points to his incomprehensible, surpassing beauty. Therefore, when I notice beauty, I deliberately turn my attention to worshipping God—declaring that he is more beautiful than anything in this world. I thank him for the beauty in this world that turns my attention to him. This discipline has kept me from letting my heart and mind wander into dangerous territory as I navigate a culture where sex and bodies are so freely displayed.

But when it comes to your spouse, let your heart delight in their physical form and the attractiveness of their personality. Celebrate who they are and affirm what you like about them, their body, and their sexuality.

I always give the following advice to newlyweds. Even though you will probably always notice younger and more attractive bodies as you age, refuse to let your heart drink in the beauty of any other person than your spouse (Proverbs 5:15, 20). Bodies change over time and usually not for the better. Every day, if you choose to delight in God's design of your spouse's body and keep your gazing eyes devoted to them alone, then your inner appreciation of beauty is more likely to evolve alongside their gradual changes.

To this day—fifteen years into marriage and even after pregnancies, injuries, and medical challenges—my wife and I let the other's body capture our attention. We playfully peek at each other in the shower or sit up in bed to watch the other undress. And this practice—alongside maintaining the righteous pathway to intimacy—has kept us attracted to each other as our bodies have aged.

Even if you're learning this advice much later in your marriage, you can begin the habit today. Your spouse is not an object to be ogled for selfish reasons, but they are a person in whom God has invited you to delight. You are gifts to each other from the Father, and you honor him by appreciating and enjoying his gift.

Especially take time to cuddle, feel, smell, and observe your spouse after sex. The oxytocin released in the body during orgasm is a powerful bonding agent. Making the most of it is healthy for the strength of the spousal relationship and will help with your ongoing connection.

Glorious Sex

As mentioned in chapter 4, sex isn't only for procreation. A person becomes one flesh with any sexual partner (1 Corinthians 6:16). Therefore, there is spiritual value in sex beyond its utility.

God designed sex as a way for husband and wife to initiate, practice, enjoy, and celebrate their ongoing intimate union. Furthermore, God designed sex to be a prophetic reminder of Christ's passion for his church, his longing to be fully and intimately known by us, and our own desperation for his return.

Sex is glorious when it points to this reality. In chapter 6, I showed you that Jesus has surrendered the fulfillment of his greatest desire—the salvation of all humanity—in the context of union with us. In the same way, glorious sex involves the husband and wife submitting the fulfillment of their greatest desires to each other. We become stewards of each other's orgasms and serve each other in love.

Anything that fits this framework of selflessness, love, and honor is welcome in the marriage bed, as long as it doesn't violate your or your spouse's conscience.

Romans 14 demonstrates that one's personal conscience matters. If you are troubled by a particular activity, don't do it. If you think it's a sin, then for you, it is (v. 14). Also, the way we talk about our liberty matters. If we disregard other people or act haphazardly about questionable activities that legitimately trouble our neighbor, we sin. How we treat people who think differently matters. If we look down on others who hold different convictions than us on questionable matters, we sin. All these actions fall short of God's glory. Accordingly, how we discuss our creative sexual ideas with our spouse also must be oriented toward loving and serving them, not selfishly indulging our own curiosity.

The lesson of Romans 14 is that each person is accountable before God on our own—both for how we honor our consciences and for how we honor the consciences of others. Therefore, we should prioritize love over liberty. In the marriage bed, your activities with each other are limited, first, by God's expressly stated biblical rules about holy sex and, second, by both of your consciences. With those constraints in effect, the marriage bed is a place of adventure and deep intimacy.

With intentionality and a commitment to God's designed pathway to intimacy, you and your spouse can have glorious sex. Even if you have physical limitations, you are limited only by selfless love, conscience, and your own creativity. You can steward your spouse's orgasm in ways that may be less conventional but are every bit as loving and selfless.

The Christian life is not a place of sexual suppression. Rather, God offers us marriage as a place to express and enjoy sex in all its sacred glory.

Gathering Your Thoughts

Write down your thoughts about these questions before talking to your spouse about this chapter. Talk to the Lord about any shortcomings you see in yourself, and simply trust him to immediately bring forgiveness, freedom, and transformation to your heart.

1. What are some realizations you had about holy sex or your current sex life as you read this chapter?
2. Ask the Lord if you have been successfully relying on him to keep you free from sinful lust. Pay attention to the thoughts and feelings that come to mind. If needed, confess your sin and consider your flesh dead on the cross. Thank Jesus for setting you free and empowering you to live differently.
3. Take time to delight in your spouse. Write him or her a note or card that expresses what you like about their personality, their body, and your sex life. If other aspects of the pathway to intimacy need to be corrected, hold off giving them this note to avoid sending a mixed signal. But when you're ready, find an appropriate time to surprise them with it.

Conversation Starters

Open up to your spouse about the following topics. Require nothing from them—only give.

1. Share what impacted you most about this chapter.
2. If you know you have used your spouse selfishly for your own gratification in any way, apologize. Express your desire to honor and love them selflessly in the future.
3. Tell your spouse what, under the best circumstances, their physical closeness and sexual intimacy means to you.

Ask your spouse the following:

1. What is one sexual encounter we've had that you consider especially meaningful, beautiful, or pleasurable to you? What specifically made it such a great experience?
2. On days when I'm more in the mood than you and hinting at sex, what feelings do you tend to have? Is there anticipation,

excitement, fear, anxiety, or guilt? A mix of these? Can I do anything to help eliminate any negative feelings or lack of clarity? Can I do anything to help you feel the same way I do?

3. What is one question you have been wanting to ask me about my views, experience, or feelings around our sexual relationship?

4. Can I do anything to make our sex life more meaningful, fulfilling, and nurturing?

CHAPTER 14:

A Life of Adventure

My PARENTS JUST CELEBRATED THEIR SIXTY-SECOND wedding anniversary, and I can confidently say they're more in love now than they've ever been. Even in their eighties, they are each other's best friends. They go on frequent dates despite a limited retirement budget—sightseeing, eating out, and visiting friends. They encourage and celebrate each other's hobbies and accomplishments. They minister to friends and strangers together. They serve their church together. In short, they're the sort of people I want to be when I grow up.

My parents have weathered a lot of storms throughout their lives. They raised four children—two boys and two girls—who are all unique, each presenting our own challenges. Together, they've endured financial struggles, medical emergencies, a life-threatening highway rollover accident, the deaths of close friends and family, and betrayal by people they loved. They've even managed career changes and transitioning to retirement.

Even with so many complicated years behind them, they don't display an ounce of bitterness or resentment. My parents treat life as an adventure to enjoy, not a burden to endure.

Adventure stories are full of peril and obstacles, but they always end with a satisfying payoff. My parents keep their eyes on the prize at the end of the journey, and it has kept them strong for decades. They trust that in all things, God is working on their behalf (Romans 8:28).

The Greatest Adventure

Every individual is called into the greatest adventure: trusting and following Jesus. Certainly, you can reach the destination of this journey even if your spouse doesn't know the Lord. But of course, we will most enjoy the road when we travel it together with the one earthly person we love most.

Marital union can make you one in flesh but not one in spirit (1 Corinthians 6:16–17). But if I am one spirit with Christ and my spouse is one spirit with Christ, then we are together one spirit through our oneness with him. Jesus prayed that we—the church—would be one just as he and the Father are one. That applies to the whole body of Christ but also to a Christian husband and a Christian wife. The only way to be truly one with each other is to both be one with him. Apart from Christ, husbands and wives are merely one flesh.

If your spouse doesn't know Jesus, then at the top of your list of priorities should be revealing Jesus to them. I don't mean that in a preachy sense but rather through love and service. Live your faith in a way that is attractive to your spouse. Be appropriately verbal about your faith, always aiming to draw your spouse closer and not push them away.

And of course, if your spouse does know Jesus, enjoy your spiritual union in Christ.

A Spirit-filled, Bible-believing, people-loving church is vital to your ongoing spiritual growth and maturity. You and your spouse may be involved in the faith community to varying degrees, and that's generally okay. If your spouse isn't as interested in attending Bible studies and prayer meetings as you are, that's okay. Church doesn't need to be a chore. If anything, I recommend finding (or starting) a healthy small group that the two of you can participate in together. Many marriages have been saved because a family of believers had close enough relationship with the couple to speak into their lives, support them in stressful and painful seasons, love them through grief, pray for them, and offer a listening ear and godly wisdom.

Find a church where you both feel connected to community—not merely a weekly meeting or religious service to simply attend but a vibrant spiritual family who loves the Lord and each other. Small group ministries are great for this.

Rhythms of Life

Over years of ministry, I've noticed a tendency for those of us who hold microphones to assume that what works for us will work for everyone. All too often, a person who reads their Bible for an hour every day will teach a roomful of others that they, too, need to set aside an hour to read every day. Or someone who wakes up at four in the morning to pray before going to the gym and then to work will teach about the value of morning devotions and self-discipline.

But then an overtired mom of a toddler, who hasn't had a full night of sleep in two years, hears that message and feels inadequate in her faith. Or a man who is more of a night owl than a morning person might feel that he missed the proper time to pray or read his Bible when he hit the snooze alarm for the eighth time. Like Pharisees, we heap heavy loads on people, assuming that our own expression of devotion ought to be followed by everyone else.

In marriage, when two personalities come together in the same home, we can likewise artificially impose our standards on each other. Many times, I've heard a wife complain that her husband doesn't pray with her. I ask, "What do you mean by *pray*?" Often, the wife's definition of prayer might be some sort of deep, contemplative, half-hour session with dim lighting and instrumental music that doesn't appeal at all to her husband. Or it might be fifteen minutes of loud spiritual warfare and exuberant praise, which runs counter to her husband's more reserved personality. Or maybe all she wants is a daily ritual where they briefly pray out loud for each other. I often reply, "Would it help you to hear that Robin and I don't do that either?"

Your preferences for your devotional life are not necessarily your spouse's preferences, and that's okay. It's great to find a common ground where you can meet with the Lord at the same time, but it's possible to relate to the Lord uniquely and still follow him together.

I have friends who practice a daily routine of reading their Bibles at the same time as their spouse and then coming together to discuss what they read. Another couple I know will pray for ten minutes separately and then ten minutes together every day. Still others pray together every morning and night. Routines are great when both people want them.

Robin and I aren't like that. For one thing, our schedules are too tumultuous for such regularity. But even when our schedules were more structured, our personalities are such that any devotional routines we tried to implement were short-lived—perhaps a week or two at the most. Instead, Robin and I pray on our own schedules and spontaneously break into prayer together as a natural part of our day as needed. We both love the Lord and each other. And we feel more spiritually connected by not imposing extrabiblical standards on each other than if we tried to force some sort of structure that God doesn't require.

Not every couple is the same. How you exercise faith together doesn't have to look like us or anyone else. You don't have to feel bad if your shared routines (or lack thereof) don't look like an ideal displayed by someone you admire. Find what honors God and works for the both of you. Then do it with all your hearts.

Money

A 2023 study published in Forbes surveyed a thousand Americans who had been divorced (or were currently going through one). At 42 percent, financial security was reported as the number-one reason these couples married, even beating companionship (39 percent) and love (36 percent). Nevertheless, financial stress ranked sixth on the list of biggest factors for divorce (24 percent) and *last* on the list of measured factors that indicate a marriage might be headed for divorce. Only 5 percent reported that their marriage was beyond hope and couldn't have been saved.[42]

In other words, while finances matter and while many have touted disagreement about money as one of the leading causes of divorce, money itself is rarely the problem. How we disagree will always be more important than the fact that we disagree. How we choose to relate to each other in difficult times is more important than the fact difficult times happen.

Thirteen years ago, Robin and I were so deep in crippling debt that we couldn't even buy groceries. Miraculously—whether

---

[42] Christy Bieber, JD, "Leading Causes Of Divorce: 43% Report Lack Of Family Support," *Forbes Advisor*, August 15, 2023, https://www.forbes.com/advisor/legal/divorce/common-causes-divorce/#less_than_5_of_divorcees_say_their_marriage_couldnt_be_saved_section.

delivered by angel or fellow Christian—groceries occasionally showed up on our doorstep when we needed them most. Robin's parents helped us whenever we asked, but we tried not to ask. They often bought us formula for our baby. It was a challenging time, but the Lord, our family, and our community of faith helped us.

When we finally hit rock bottom, we made big changes in our stewardship of God's money. We stopped giving God a token 10 percent and instead dedicated 100 percent of our resources to the Lord. We started obeying him with whatever we had—often being generous beyond our means. Seven years later, we were completely debt free and started saving for the house where we now live.

A lifestyle of complete surrender to Jesus's lordship has done more for our finances than anything else. We save as he leads us, spend as he leads us, and give as he leads us. In the absence of directly hearing his voice, we exercise the wisdom, love, and generosity he has given us.

Robin and I have a set amount of money that either of us can give away to someone in need without asking the other. Amounts bigger than that require a conversation, but we almost always do it. We've never regretted being too generous.

We operate on a principle that we refuse to buy anything that we're not willing to give away if the Lord asks it from us—and that includes our cars and house. God is a good Father who can be trusted, and he has never steered us wrong.

Today, we are thriving. We support missionaries and give to people in our church who have needs. We are generous in budgeted ways and spontaneous ways. We didn't wait until we were thriving to start giving. Instead, we stewarded God's resources when we had a little, and now he can trust us with more.

Do your habits with money indicate Jesus's lordship? If not, seek the Lord about what adjustments you can make. Perhaps start by regularly giving to your local church, if you're not already.

Your desire for greater generosity doesn't have to become a fight with your spouse. Some people hoard because they feel insecure. They can't look outward because of fear. But survival mode is unbelief. It indicates more trust in *what* we have than *who* we have. How can you communicate commitment and security to your spouse so that risk becomes easier for them? Grow in your relationships with each other and the Lord, and revisit the conversation later from a place of increased faith.

Collaborate with your spouse about money. Communicate as much as is helpful. Set goals together that are consistent with Jesus's dreams for your marriage. Enjoy what God has entrusted to you until he requests or demands it from you. Joy is always on the other side of generosity.

Weathering Storms

Money isn't the only challenge we face in the adventure of marriage. Sometimes the hero's journey is plagued with peril and tragic loss.

My friends Mike and Margie always wanted children but couldn't conceive. One day, a stranger walked up to Margie in a store and daringly prophesied, "The Lord says you're going to have two children, first a boy and then a girl."

The couple held onto that promise for years but still couldn't conceive. Finally, they decided to fulfill their desire for children by becoming foster parents.

In the process, they took in a beautiful little girl who had been in a difficult home situation. They quickly fell in love with her and started the process of adopting.

Meanwhile, they took in a little boy and felt the same connection with him. They began the adoption process with him too.

Even though they started with the girl first, the boy's adoption was finalized before hers. Immediately, Margie remembered the word she was given in the store: first a boy, then a girl. Mike and Margie knew they had received the Lord's promise.

Tragically, Mike and Margie both lost their lives to cancer when the kids were in their teens. But both stood by each other and loved their kids to the best of their ability until the very end.

Infertility, miscarriages, medical emergencies, chronic conditions, terminal illness, and tragic loss are unfortunately part of this fallen world. If God wanted any of those things to happen, then he wouldn't have sent his Son to destroy the devil's work (1 John 3:8). And he wouldn't have commissioned his church to freely distribute his love, power, and grace (Matthew 10:8; John 14:12; Mark 16:17–18; 2 Corinthians 5:11–21).

Life rarely goes the way we want or expect. Marriage isn't about living happily ever after. The real world usually looks less like all our dreams coming true and more like shattered dreams and crushing heartache. Marriage is about consistently loving someone in a way that reveals Jesus and the church in the face of such great trials. It's an opportunity to stand with and support someone else, feeling what they feel because you're also deeply impacted by your shared struggle. In that place, our love and commitment to each other and our faith in God can shine gloriously.

Parenting

Parenting deserves a book all its own, but for the purposes of the message at hand, simply know that how you and your spouse reveal Jesus will be most acutely felt by your children. So, often, our experiences with parents influence our understanding of God, for better or worse.

Anytime I've responded to my children in my flesh, I apologize to them. I say, "Sorry, son. That wasn't Jesus. Jesus is like this . . ." So not only do I model how to identify sin and apologize, it also becomes a learning opportunity about the Lord. Soon, my kids start to catch on to what Jesus is like. A couple of times, they've called me out, saying, "I don't think this is Jesus, Dad." Over time, I've grown significantly, and such apologies are needed less often.

But remember that Jesus isn't a pushover. He still confronts sin. He's gracious, giving us room to grow and discover truth. He opposes pride and rewards trust and humility. "The Lord disciplines the one he loves, and he chastens everyone he accepts as his son" (Hebrews 12:6). Discipline and correction are part of a healthy home.

God also listens to us. He pays close enough attention to our situation to truly understand us. And with full knowledge of what transpired, he perfectly exercises the right balance of compassion and accountability, helping us live rightly next time.

Anytime you're wondering what to do as you're raising kids, simply observe the Father. How does he raise us? What does he want to do in this specific situation. Ask him for wisdom, and he will give it. Everything I shared in previous chapters about attachment styles, triggers, and sinful judgments applies in our parenting relationship as well.

Communicate with your spouse regularly about your children. Present a united, consistent response to their behaviors. If one parent says no, both parents say no. Support each other and stand up for each other in love. Let your oneness demonstrate the gospel to your kids.

Also, shower them with affection and affirmation. Bless them. Pray out loud for them. Robin and I determined that we wanted the atmosphere of our home to be so filled with the presence of God that when our children experienced anything different, they would notice and feel uncomfortable. If you want your kids to feel at home in heaven, then welcome heaven into your home.

Transitions

I like to joke that in my early twenties, I thought I had been fully sanctified. All my issues were crucified, and I was a living, breathing revelation of Jesus.

And then I got married.

Then, just as our emotional and spiritual wrinkles were getting ironed out, we had a baby.

Then we had another.

Then I started a church.

Every step of the way, new relational responsibilities exposed new insecurities and helped me discover that I wasn't as sanctified as I thought.

Every time you put an addition on a house, you have to dig a new foundation for the extension. You may have done plenty of digging—identifying past traumas, forgiving offenders, repenting of sinful judgments and lies believed, and crucifying sin—and you may have reached a place of equilibrium where you feel stable in your faith and relationships. But if you want to add a new relationship, role, career, ministry, or other opportunity, expect to unearth new skeletons as you dig in areas you never previously needed to address.

Some people expect transitions to save them out of struggles. Certainly, sometimes a change of career or a move into a new home can be a breath of fresh air. But more often than we would like to admit, the problem wasn't our circumstances—it was us.

As it turns out, wherever you go, there you are. If you keep moving from one job to the next, one church to the next, one community to the next, and so on, searching for peace, you'll never find it. Don't put your hope in transitions; put your hope in the Lord. Learn what it means to be free *before* your circumstances change.

Scripture is full of examples of people's lives going in unexpected directions. A prime example is Joseph. He had a dream that God would make him important, but his brothers sold him into slavery and faked his death. Nevertheless, Joseph remained faithful to the Lord. He kept his integrity. Even wrongfully accused and thrown into prison, he maintained the freedom in his heart, interpreting dreams and being a model prisoner. Joseph was free in his spirit even before he was free from his situation, and eventually, he became second-in-command in Egypt and rescued God's people from a massive famine (Genesis 37–47).

You don't have to chase after dreams. Seek first God's kingdom, and he'll take care of everything else (Matthew 6:33). That means you don't have to chase transitions as your source of happiness. Learn to be happy where you are and take transitions as they come. As Paul said in Philippians 4:12–13, "I know what it is to be in need, and I know what it is to have plenty. I have learned the secret of being content in any and every situation, whether well fed or hungry, whether living in plenty or in want. I can do all this through him who gives me strength."

Ministry

You don't have to be a pastor to be in ministry. Every Christian is commissioned to be a disciple of Jesus who makes more disciples for him (Matthew 28:19–20). If you and your spouse are following Jesus together, that means you can make disciples together.

Find one or more people who haven't known the Lord as long as you, and invite them to spend regular time in your home. If you and your spouse are displaying Jesus in your marriage even to a fraction of what I've shared in this book, your time will be well spent. Mentor them. Pray for them. Above all, point them to Jesus so they depend more on him than on you.

Volunteer in your church. You and your spouse may find a place to serve together, or you might find unrelated roles to fill. Either way, serving the same vision can be great for your sense of shared success.

Too many wives of male pastors are expected to fill stereotypical roles—like leading the women's ministry or children's ministry or, in some churches, even preaching and teaching. If that's your calling, do what God has called you to do. But never feel pressured to step outside your own unique gifts and personality to please people or meet unrealistic expectations. Feel free to be you.

Scripture talks about spiritual gifts—special abilities that the Holy Spirit gives so God's people can love and serve each other beyond our human ability (Romans 12:6–8; 1 Corinthians 12:1–11; 1 Peter 4:10–11). Your dominant spiritual gifts and ministry strengths are likely different from your spouse's, but since the Holy Spirit distributes such abilities according to his wisdom, those gifts are also likely complementary. Over time, figure out how you and your spouse are most impactful together. Don't feel like you need to measure up to your spouse in their abilities. Be uniquely you. Together, the two of you will present a fuller revelation of Jesus than either of you could have on your own.

Vision for the Future

God designed your marriage to shine in the darkness. It's an adventure full of twists, turns, tragedies, and triumphs.

How do you think about the past? Do you view it with regret and frustration? Or do you see the Lord's hand bringing you through the mess to where you are today? How we frame our past will influence how we endure the present and look to the future. Rather than focusing on all the challenges that seemed to derail your destiny, focus on the Lord and his faithfulness to redeem it all. If he has brought you this far, he will take you further.

As you go throughout life, it's good to work on your relationship. But define your goals. Inward goals—like happiness—may keep you trapped in an endless cycle of reading marriage books and going to counseling sessions, seeking after a specific feeling that may never come. Outward goals—like obeying Jesus and engaging in his mission—will keep you from being ineffective in your marriage.

What is your vision for the future? What are you expecting God to do? Jesus offered his disciples a realistic expectation when he said, "In this world you will have trouble. But take heart! I have overcome the world" (John 16:33). If your vision is worldly happiness—a better job, a bigger house, a higher income, less complicated relationships, etc.—then you may achieve some relief from time to time, but you'll probably be mostly frustrated. But if your vision is to be conformed into the image and likeness of Jesus, then it doesn't matter what life throws at you. You can stand firm, knowing that Jesus has the victory already procured, and you are daily looking more like him.

Every great adventure story ends with victory. The treasure is found, the loved one is rescued, the enemy is defeated, and the dragon is slain. If you're following Jesus, then the victorious end of your story is already written. You can throw yourself into great risk—loving deeply and living fully—knowing that your good and perfect Father will guide you through to your eternity with him.

Gathering Your Thoughts

Write down your thoughts about these questions before talking to your spouse about this chapter. Talk to the Lord about any shortcomings you see in yourself, and simply trust him to immediately bring forgiveness, freedom, and transformation to your heart.

1. Have you and your spouse endured any setbacks or tragedies in the past? What do you think about these experiences? Do you focus more on the problem or on the Lord's redemptive work? Ask the Lord if he wants to show you anything about his faithfulness, love, and victory that might redeem how you view each past struggle.
2. Have you been unnecessarily pressuring your spouse to live up to your preferences in any areas, such as their prayer habits, devotional life, or ministry activities? Write these down and let the Lord adjust your heart to grant freedom and choice to your spouse.
3. Ask the Lord to give you his heart for your marriage, and then write down what you feel God wants for your future together. Be cautious not to slip into the trap of defining who you wish your spouse would be. Instead, write about the person you already know them to be, the potential you already see in the two of you, and the sort of impact you would love to make and legacy you would like to leave for your children and in the world. Take time to pray that God would work out his vision for your marriage.

Conversation Starters

Open up to your spouse about the following topics. Require nothing from them—only give.

1. Share what impacted you most about this chapter.
2. Apologize for any areas where you have unnecessarily pressured your spouse to live up to a particular standard that was out of line with God's design for their life. Verbally give them liberty in how they pursue God and minister to others.
3. Speak a blessing over your spouse. This generally looks something like, "In the name of Jesus, I bless and affirm you

as my spouse. May you experience [list some good things you desire for your spouse]. And may I [list some ways you want to be a blessing to your spouse]." Speak words of love, affirmation, and admiration that convey the trust that you have chosen to place in your spouse and that express how you value them.

Ask your spouse the following:

1. Are there any areas of our marriage where you don't feel we're walking in unity?
2. What do you feel God might want for our future together as a couple/family?

Conclusion

A S MENTIONED IN THE FINAL CHAPTER, MY PARENTS, Gaylord and Linda Thomas, have been married sixty-two years. I asked them what advice they would like to offer you as the reader, and it's my joy to present their words to you here.

My eighty-two-year-old dad's immediate response was, "Always be each other's best friend, and keep the romance alive. Successful marriage is constant caring—aiming to make the other person's day the best it can possibly be. For me, your mom is first, and for her, I am first. And, of course, what we have going for us is that Jesus is number one. As the Lord is number one in both of your lives, then the three of you become one. The three of us are constantly looking out for each other.

"It's a wonderful life. I just can't get over what a wonderful wife I have and all that she does for me, so I try to do as much as I can for her. I see little things I can do so she has time to do the things she wants to do and vice versa. It can't be only one day; it has to be every day. I wake up in the morning and pray, 'Lord, order my steps, and help me be the best husband I can possibly be.'"

Mom added, "You have to overlook things that you don't think are right, because if you look at those things all the time and not at the person you married, you're going to be miserable. I went through that stage for a time, but then I decided that rather than curse our marriage, I would bless it. It truly helps stabilize the marriage when you prioritize oneness of heart, rather than putting up walls over petty offenses."

In 2019, my mom was in the hospital with her organs failing. The doctors had no idea what was happening. At one point, she died. She said her spirit could see her body, and over to one side, she saw Jesus, sword in hand, fighting a large, billowing black cloud. She cried out, "Help me, Jesus! Help me, Jesus!"

Mom said that Jesus stopped fighting and turned to look at her with his hand on his hip, as if to ask, "What do you think I'm doing?"

After a couple of repetitions of this same exchange, my mom said she finally realized she wasn't supposed to fight but to trust. She shocked the nurses when she returned to life without their intervention.

Soon after that, Mom was released from the hospital but still had to have kidney dialysis. Three times each week, Dad would help her to the car and drive her twenty-five miles to the clinic for her four-hour treatment. Dad made a CD of songs that he and my mom used to dance to in his parents' basement when they were dating, transferring them from his old reel-to-reel tape player so she could listen during her stay.

Dad said, "Instead of complaining about the inconvenience of the treatment, we made the best of it. Afterward, I'd ask her if she wanted to go out to eat, and we'd make a date out of it. We have an attitude that we're not going to let anything get us down."

Dad would still be doing all that, but after only ten weeks, my mom's kidneys miraculously recovered, and she hasn't needed dialysis since. Today, almost five years later, her kidney function continues to improve, and she knows the Lord has healed her. My parents have demonstrated this sort of steadfast love for sixty-two years—through good times and bad—and are today displaying a prophetic picture of Jesus and his bride.

My wife and I have been transformed by the gospel, displayed by our parents and taught through various pastors, preachers, and authors—especially in the Bible. The good news of what Jesus has done has changed us as individuals and as a couple. There is no greater message to which you can devote your life.

Your marriage matters to God. It's a perfect covenant that he established and blessed. It is a prophetic message that has been entrusted to you and your spouse.

Conclusion

May God open the eyes of your hearts to see him more clearly, know him more fully, and be transformed more into his image and likeness. May your marriage be glorious, displaying the splendor of the pure and spotless bride and Bridegroom.

Like my parents, always be each other's best friend. No matter how challenging life becomes, remember that marriage is for displaying Jesus to each other and the world. Whatever your next season holds, Jesus is with you. Remember that the gospel is the solution to every problem. Because of what Jesus has done, there is good news for your marriage.

www.ingramcontent.com/pod-product-compliance
Lightning Source LLC
Chambersburg PA
CBHW051419090426
42737CB00014B/2743